THE REMINISCENCES

OF

JAMES BURRILL ANGELL

James B. Angell

THE
REMINISCENCES
OF
JAMES BURRILL ANGELL

BOOKS FOR LIBRARIES PRESS
FREEPORT, NEW YORK

First Published 1911
Reprinted 1971

INTERNATIONAL STANDARD BOOK NUMBER:
0-8369-5722-9

LIBRARY OF CONGRESS CATALOG CARD NUMBER:
79-152970

PRINTED IN THE UNITED STATES OF AMERICA

PREFACE

MANY of my friends can bear witness that it is not without a certain reluctance that I have prepared this volume of Reminiscences for publication. I have done it under the pressure of frequent and urgent requests from colleagues in the Faculties, and from students of the three Universities, with which I have been officially connected. They have thought that many of the facts which I have described in my narrative are worthy of being recorded in a permanent form.

I venture to hope that the narrative may prove of interest to them. I can assure them, however, that autobiography compels one to write so largely of one's self that it involves the serious discomfort of a seeming lack of modesty. But that discomfort will be cheerfully borne by the writer, if this volume shall help to keep him in touch with the colleagues and students whose friendship has brought so much joy into his life.

UNIVERSITY OF MICHIGAN,
    July 1, 1911.

CONTENTS

[vii]

REMINISCENCES OF
JAMES B. ANGELL

I

FROM BIRTH TO GRADUATION
1829-1849

I WAS born in Scituate, Rhode Island, on January 7, 1829. My parents were Andrew Aldrich Angell and Amy Aldrich Angell. They were remotely related. I am the oldest of eight children, two of whom died in infancy. I am the lineal descendant, of the seventh generation, from Thomas Angell who, an Englishman by birth, came, in 1631, to Massachusetts with Roger Williams, and, in 1636, accompanied Williams when the latter settled on the spot to which he gave the name of Providence. Thomas Angell was one of the signers of the noted compact[1] to which

[1] This is the Compact. "We whose names are hereunder written, being desirous to inhabit in the town of Providence, do promise to submit ourselves in active or passive obedience, to all such orders or agreements as shall be made for public good of the body, in an orderly way, by the major consent of the present inhabitants, masters of families incorporated together into a township, and such others whom they shall admit into the same, *only in civil things*." Signed by thirteen persons.

[1]

Rhode Islanders have always looked back with pride, as the first instrument of pure democracy, which leaves absolute freedom in matters of religious concern.

In 1675, as is learned from the Providence Early Records, lands on the west side of the so-called Seven Mile Line were assigned to several men. Among them was Thomas Angell. His grandson and namesake, Thomas, appears to have settled in 1710 on the farm on which I was born.

The town was incorporated in 1731. Why the name Scituate was given to it is not clear. It has been thought by some it was because it was partly settled by emigrants from Scituate, Massachusetts. But I have never heard of but one settler from that place. We know that the Massachusetts antiquarians believe that the name is Indian, being written Setuat, or nearly in that form, and signifying Cold Brooks.[1] It is not improbable that the site of the town in Rhode Island bore a similar Indian name, and was anglicized like that in Massachusetts by the form Scituate.

The land, or a portion of it, on which Thomas settled, was held and occupied continuously by his descendants until after the death of my father in 1864. Repre-

[1] "Mass. Hist. Coll.," Second Series, Vol. 4, p. 223.

sentatives of the Angell family are numerous in Rhode Island, where in the main they have remained. They have been found chiefly in the ranks of plain farmers, mechanics and tradesmen, gaining by industry and integrity an honest living, but winning no particular distinction. Those best known, perhaps, are Col. Israel Angell, who commanded in a creditable manner a regiment in the Revolution, and Joseph Kinnicutt Angell, whose books on law gave him some eminence in the last generation. Nearly always some of them have been found in the State Legislature.

My immediate ancestors, like many of the farmers of former days who lived on some important thoroughfare, combined the business of tavern-keeping with that of farming. At an early day the Providence and Norwich Turnpike Company, whose road passed through our farm, was chartered. The farmers of several towns in eastern Connecticut then marketed their products in Providence and so travelled the turnpike road. During the War of 1812, much of the travel and transportation by land between Boston and New York went by this route. Good inns were therefore needed. Through the period of my boyhood the number of travellers who sought accommodations in the spacious house which my grandfather erected in 1810, was very considerable. In earlier days, the town meetings were held at the tavern. In my own time, the military gatherings—the "General Trainings"—were held in the intervales near by; political meetings, occasionally a justice's court, were held in a large hall which formed a part of the house. Compared with the seclusion of the ordinary farmer's boy's life, it will readily be seen that life here was very stirring. I have always felt that the knowledge of men I gained by the observations and experiences of my boyhood in the country tavern has been of the greatest service. Human nature could be studied in every variety, from that of the common farm labourer to travellers of the highest breeding and refinement. The eminent political speakers were always entertained at our table, and some of them were very helpful friends in my later life. If, as I have sometimes been assured, I have any power of adaptation to the society of different classes of men, I owe it in no small degree to these varied associations of my boyhood.

I began my education by learning my alphabet from an old law book. My grandfather had been Justice of the Peace, and therefore had this volume, each chapter of which began with a very large capital letter. Under the guidance of my uncle, I learned these letters. That fact is my earliest recollection. I recall with especial distinctness the large J, as I was made to understand that it was the initial of my name.

I may remark in passing that my name was given me by my step-grandfather, who was an admirer of James Burrill,[1] an early United States Senator from Rhode Island.

At a very early age (I know not how early), I was sent to the District School. I remember that I was so young that my father used frequently to take me to school on horseback in front of him on the saddle. A large boy of the neighbourhood was hired to take charge of me on the road when I walked. The district school was then in a very primitive state. A sloping board attached to the wall quite around the room was the writing desk for all the larger pupils. They sat on benches with their backs towards the middle of the room. The small scholars sat on low benches in the centre of the room. Those who wrote

[1] He was the grandfather of George William Curtis and Rev. James Burrill Curtis. Hence George Curtis used playfully to call me his cousin.

made their own writing books. They purchased unruled paper, cut it into leaves,
stitched them together, put a rough brown
paper cover on, and ruled the lines with a
leaden plummet. The first duty in the
morning was to mend the goose-quill pens,
and in the winter to thaw the ink on the
stove. The highest branch was Daboll's
Arithmetic, and the older pupils who had
completed it one winter came back the
next and "ciphered through it" again.
Reading, spelling, writing, a little grammar,
elementary geography, and arithmetic, furnished the whole curriculum.

Fortunately for me, when I was about
eight years of age a Quaker, Isaac Fiske,
came to the neighbourhood, and established
a school for boarders and for day scholars,
and I was placed under his care. He was a
most thorough, painstaking, and exacting
teacher. He had little class-work. His
instruction was personal. He went round
from pupil to pupil to render needed assistance in solving mathematical problems.
When we had completed them he required
us to copy our work neatly into manuscript
books. I remained with him four years,
and not only completed arithmetic, but
studied surveying also. As he did not
teach foreign languages, ancient or modern,

he advised my parents to place me in some school where I might study Latin. But, for the thoroughness of his instruction I have always felt under deep obligations to him.

Some boys whom I knew were attending a seminary in Seekonk, Massachusetts, about three miles from Providence, and urged me to come there. It was a great trial to my mother to have me leave home; but it was decided that I ought to go. I was then twelve years old. On arriving at the school, I found that in arithmetic I was far ahead of the boys of my age, and so it was wisely concluded that I should give my whole time to Latin. And this experiment of intensive study, carried on in a rational way, had a very interesting result. The principal put me in charge of his sister, a very intelligent woman. He had been drilling a class of older boys two years on the dry rules of Latin grammar, without letting them read much Latin. The sister gave me a small book containing the paradigms and easy reading lessons. I met her twice a day, finished the book, and by the end of the three months' term was able to join the class of older boys in such reading as was then set for them, and to go on with them without difficulty.

[7]

After I had spent one term at this school, my parents decided to send me to the Smithville Seminary, an Academy which the Freewill Baptists had established in the northern part of my own town, only five miles from my home.

The two principal instructors, Rev. Hosea Quinby, a graduate of Waterville College, Maine, and Mr. S. L. Weld, a graduate of Brown University, were familiar with the traditional methods of the New England Academy. Without being eminent scholars, they had the faculty of interesting, and to a fair degree of stimulating, their pupils. Most of these were farmers' sons and daughters who wished to supplement the limited work of the district schools. A small number were preparing themselves for college. I joined them in their classes with no such purpose distinctly formed. I also took nearly all the scientific instruction which was given, and given as well as it could be without laboratories or much apparatus. Many of the students were men in years. They were diligent students. Some of them were awkward and rustic in manners, but they were thoroughly earnest and gave a good tone to the school.

The best instruction, and that was the case in such schools generally, was in mathematics. I pushed on through algebra and plane and solid geometry. English was taught by the stupid method of parsing "Pope's Essay on Man" and that dolorous book, "Pollock's Course of Time." The ideals of writing and speaking which were in vogue were greatly wanting in simplicity and directness. The instruction in the classics, while it would not now be regarded as sufficiently critical, encouraged and enabled us to read rapidly enough to get real enjoyment from the author. We soon caught the swing and the flow of the Virgilian verse, so that we read with genuine delight in the last six books of the Æneid at the rate of three hundred lines a day. The poem was not made a mere frame-work on which to hang puzzling questions in grammar, but read as a poem which we were to enjoy as we did Scott's "Marmion" or the "Lady of the Lake." That method may be deemed old-fashioned by modern doctors of philosophy; but I have always been very grateful that under that method my first acquaintance with Virgil was not dull task-work, but the source of constant delight.

As I look back on the work done in the dead or moribund academies of New England which have been supplanted by the well-appointed high school, I am convinced that, with their many defects, due in large part to inadequate means, they rendered a most valuable service. They prepared teachers for the district schools, young men for business, and a limited number to meet the moderate requirements which were asked in that time for admission to college. We are in danger of underrating the value of their work.

While during my fourteenth year I was at school at the Academy, Mr. O. S. Fowler, a somewhat noted phrenologist of that day, gave some lectures in the village of North Scituate and made a professional "examination" of my head. I still have his written report on me. It was ridiculous in its exaggerated estimate of my gifts, but it had one good result. He persuaded my relatives and friends that by study I was overtaxing my strength, and that I ought to leave school for a time and lead a vigorous out-of-door life. While I was by no means ill, I have little doubt that I owe in some degree the physical vigour with which I have been blessed all my life to the fact that owing to his counsel I spent the next two seasons, from early spring till late autumn, at work upon my father's farm, side by side with his hired men, hoeing my row and mowing my swath and learning all the details of farm work. Much of this I had previously learned in vacations; but I now learned thoroughly how much backache a dollar earned in the fields represented. I was also enabled to see how the world looks from the point of view of the labouring man. Often in later years, when weary with study, I was inspired with new zeal by recalling how much severer were the fatigue and monotony of the work of the farmer's boy. It is a good fortune for a boy to have known by experience what hard and continuous manual labour means.

The life in my native town during the years of my boyhood was much like that in the other rural towns of Rhode Island. It was very simple and frugal. The population was of pure English descent. I think my father within the period of my recollection brought the first Irish maid-servant into the town. Farming was the chief occupation. There were half-a-dozen cotton factories of moderate size scattered through the town; but the operatives were drawn from the farms and were all Americans. The farmers got their limited supply of money from the sale chiefly of wood, charcoal, and potatoes, in Providence, and of milk and butter to the operatives in the mills. Some added to their income by

turning bobbins and spools in the winter
in small shops erected on little streams upon
their farms. They found a ready market
for their products in the cotton factories
through the State. The practice of the
greatest economy was necessary to make a
small farm support a family. In 1840 the
census-taker permitted me to accompany
him in his gig over a large part of the town.
I think we entered only two or three houses
which had any other carpets or rugs than
those which the occupants had made from
rags. I believe that there were not more
than two pianos in the town. There was
no public library; there were very few
books in private libraries. Although the
town was only twelve miles from Brown
University, I was the first boy from Scituate to graduate from the college. But
there had always been in the town some men
of prominence in public affairs. Stephen
Hopkins, the signer of the Declaration of
Independence, lived there. In my own
time, one governor of the State and one
lieutenant-governor resided there; but
the great mass of the inhabitants were
hard-working farmers, who led toilsome,
honest lives, and left little to their children
beyond the inheritance they had received
from their parents. If the children were

now willing to practise the same industry
and frugality they could live with equal
comfort upon the farms. But they are
rapidly selling them to the Irish and the
French, who are willing to practise even
greater economy than the fathers did two
generations back, and so are living in comparative thrift. The change in the type of
population is marked, as it is in most of
the rural towns of New England, perhaps
even more so, since the operatives in the
factories are now almost all of foreign
birth.

The amusements of the country folk were
few and simple. Perhaps the most generally attractive was the annual visit to
the shore of Narragansett Bay, usually at
a place called the Buttonwoods, where,
under the shade of some sycamore trees,
they made a clambake after the manner
of the Indians. They first gathered the
clams from the sand laid bare by the reced-
ing tide or the quahog from the adjacent
waters. They built a fire on stones and
heated them thoroughly; and then placing
the shell-fish and potatoes and ears of corn
on the stones they covered the whole with
sea-weed, and the cooking was slowly done.
While the roasting was going on, a bath in
the sea was enjoyed by all who wished it.

The clam or quahog, held in the hand, was dipped in a cup of melted butter and eaten with a relish which no participant in one of those out-of-door feasts will ever forget.

Every farmer was expected to take his family and his hired men "to the shore" at least once, when the haying season was over. At the time of the August full moon the roads were well filled with these pilgrims to the sea. Occasionally a party of neighbours, numbering fifteen or twenty, hired a large sail boat at Apponaug or East Greenwich, and after the clambake sailed down the bay to Hope Island, spent the night there, and rose at dawn to fish. Occasionally the dullness of the winter was enlivened by a ball at some one of the taverns in the town; but the life was upon the whole monotonous, and constant toil was relieved by few amusements.

Probably, owing to the reaction among the early settlers of Rhode Island from the Puritanical spirit of their neighbours in Massachusetts and Connecticut, Sunday was not generally kept as it was in those States. It was the day for visiting relatives and friends and largely for fishing and hunting and ball-playing. It may truthfully be said that the factory operatives had no other time for visiting or for pleasure.

The most numerous religious bodies in our part of the State were the Six Principle Baptists and the Freewill Baptists. The preachers of the former denomination were all men of limited education; so were most of the preachers of the latter. Naturally enough, the men of the most intelligence and influence rarely attended church, and the spiritual life of the town was at a rather low ebb. But the general standard of morals would compare well with that of the present day. Drunkenness and gambling were not prevalent. A man supposed to be addicted to gambling or to licentiousness could not retain the public esteem. Political life was purer than it has been of late years in the State.

The language of the people retained some peculiar expressions which must have come from England, and which I have heard rarely or not at all in other parts of our country. Thus after a wedding it was customary for the parents of the bride to give a party. That party was always spoken of as the *onfare*. Whether that is the proper spelling I cannot say, as I never saw it in print. It would *seem* to come from the word fare in the sense to travel. The occasion was, therefore, a sort of God-speed, to send the married couple faring on their way.

Again, if a candidate for office was going about, buttonholing men and soliciting support, he was said to be "parmateering." It has occurred to me that that word might be an abbreviation of *Parliamenteering*, if that form was ever used to signify going about seeking support for parliament. An auction was generally spoken of as a *vendue*, pronounced *vandue*. That word borrowed from the French was used in England.

Up to the time I left the Academy I had no fixed plan for life. My teachers had encouraged me to believe that I could succeed in college studies. But, although at the age of fourteen I had covered more ground, especially in Latin and mathematics, than was required for admission to any of the New England colleges, I had no definite purpose of going to college. During the summers I was at home on the farm. I made some unsuccessful efforts to secure a clerkship in business establishments in Providence; but in my fifteenth year it was clear that I ought to decide what career I should endeavour to follow. My father informed me that he was able and willing to send me to college, but in that case would hardly be able, in justice to my five brothers and sisters, to aid me further.

It was left to me to say whether I should go. I was certain that it would gratify both him and my mother if I chose to take the college life, and so the die was cast.

Conscious that in my somewhat prolonged absence from school my knowledge of the classics had become rather rusty, and being still a year below the age set for entering Brown University, I spent the larger part of a school year in the University Grammar School in Providence. It was then conducted by Mr. Merrick Lyon and Mr. Henry S. Frieze, afterwards the distinguished Professor of Latin in the University of Michigan. My studies were mainly in the classes of the latter. Contact with this inspiring teacher formed an epoch in my intellectual life, as in that of so many other boys. He represented the best type of the modern teacher, at once critical as a grammarian and stimulating with the finest appreciation of whatever was choicest in the classic masterpieces. At first, as we were showered with questions such as I had never heard before, it seemed to me, although the reading of the Latin was mainly a review to me, that I should never emerge from my state of ignorance. But there was such a glow of enthusiasm in the instructor and in the class, there was such delight in the tension in which we were kept by the daily exercises, that no task seemed too great to be encountered. Though in conjunction with our reading we devoured the Latin grammar so that by the end of the year we could repeat almost the whole of it, paradigms, rules, and exceptions without prompting, the work of mastering it did not seem dry and onerous, for we now felt how the increasing accuracy of our knowledge of the structure of the language enhanced our enjoyment of the Virgil and the Cicero, whose subtle and less obvious charms we were aided by our teacher to appreciate.

I here interrupt the sketch of my education in school to speak of an important event in 1842, which awakened a deep and a permanent interest in me in political and constitutional questions: I refer to what is known in Rhode Island history as the Dorr war.

Rhode Island retained the very liberal charter she had received from Charles II as her Constitution down to 1843. Under that Constitution the right of suffrage was limited to the owners of land of the value of at least one hundred and thirty-four dollars and to the oldest sons of such landholders. So long as the people of the State were engaged mainly in farming, in com-

merce and in whale fishing, there was no
serious discontent with this limitation of the
suffrage. But after the War of 1812, manufacturing, especially the manufacture of
cotton, grew up rapidly in the State. By
1840 the operatives and the mechanics in
the State, who had no right to vote, were
a numerous body. Naturally enough they
sought an amendment to the Constitution
which would permit them to have a voice
in choosing their rulers; but they sought
in vain. There, as everywhere, the exclu-
sive possessors of power preferred to retain
it. Therefore the petitioners, seeing no
possibility of securing an amendment to the
constitution in accordance with the method
provided by it, called a convention to frame
such a constitution as they desired, nominated officers to be voted for at the same
time the constitution was submitted to be
adopted or rejected by those on whom this
new constitution conferred the privilege of
suffrage. The supporters of the State government mainly absented themselves from
the polls. The new constitution was declared by its friends to be adopted. Thomas
W. Dorr, a most worthy and capable man,
belonging to one of the most respectable
families of Providence, was said to be elected
governor. He at once laid claim to the

office and demanded possession of the State property. Then his subordinate officers attempted to take possession. Governor King resisted, and so an armed conflict came on. Those who supported the regular State authorities were known as the Law and Order Party, and the opponents as the Dorrites.

I am not to recite the detailed history of the strife, which resulted in the defeat of the Dorrites and in the trial, conviction, and imprisonment of Mr. Dorr on the charge of treason. It also led the victors to see that the time had come for enlarging the suffrage. They made a new and more liberal constitution, under which by the payment of a small registry or poll tax the suffrage was opened to all citizens of American birth.

But the issue which was raised by the original contest was one of great constitutional interest and importance and was made so plain that we schoolboys could comprehend it clearly enough to discuss it in our essays and debates in school, though I believe great constitutional lawyers are not yet fully agreed upon the decision of the fundamental question involved. The question is whether the citizens of a State have a right to call a convention and adopt a constitution by any other method than that prescribed in the Constitution already in force. This was, of course, decided in the negative in Rhode Island.

The feeling of opposition between the two parties in the state was almost as acute as that between the Union men and the Confederates in the Border States during the Civil War. My father was a Law and Order man, and a member of the Legislature during the troubles. The people who lived near us in the adjoining factory village were all Dorrites. They gave us to understand that they would not aid us to extinguish the flames if our house took fire. We happened to be building a large addition to our kitchen that year. They dubbed it the Algerine kitchen, as their favourite name for their opponents was Algerines, because of the alleged cruelty of the State officials towards the prisoners they took. The family adopted the name for the kitchen, and it was known as "the Algerine" so long as the house stood. As in the South after the Civil War, the women retained their animosities much longer than the men. The Dorr War affected permanently the political division of men in the State. The Democrats in other States generally sympathized with Mr. Dorr. Therefore most of the Rhode Island Democrats (of whom my father was one) who opposed him, and they were numerous, subsequently acted with the Whig party during the remaining years of the existence of that party. I therefore grew up with an inherited attachment to the Whigs, save that like most of the Brown University students I was led by President Wayland's instructions to doubt the wisdom or justice of protective tariffs.

My college life covered the period from 1845 to 1849. In these days, when the faculty numbers nearly a hundred, it is difficult to comprehend how a faculty of seven men carried on the institution with vigour and success. I need hardly say that each one of the seven was a man of force and was admirably qualified for his special work.

The youngest was Professor Lincoln. He had recently returned from Germany, where he had pursued extended studies in the classics and in philosophy. We had the pleasure of reading Livy with him while he was preparing his edition of that author. He was, therefore, brimful of enthusiasm on the subject and fired us with much of his own spirit. Although we were studying a dead language, no classroom was more alive than this. He was intolerant of sluggishness or laziness, and often rebuked it with a stinging word. "I have forgotten," said an indolent fellow one day in reply to a question. "Forgotten," was the sharp retort of the teacher, "did you ever know?" One answer given him amused him and the class as affording rich material for his notes on Livy. We were reading the twenty-first chapter, which describes the passage of the Alps by Hannibal. The professor asked one of the class why Hannibal had the elephants with him. With great promptness the answer came, "to draw up his cannon." The youth who made the reply was so chaffed by his classmates that he left Brown and went to another college.

Professor Boise, who afterwards at the University of Michigan and the Chicago Theological Seminary won so high a reputation, had charge of the Greek. He manifested the same philological acumen which always distinguished him. But he seemed to us at that time to dwell too much on the minutiæ of grammar, and not enough on the beauties of Greek literature. The current saying among us was that "he would die for an enclitic." But it is impossible to overstate the influence which he and his colleague, Professor Frieze, exerted in the West through their labours at the University of Michigan in diffusing love for the study of the ancient classics.

The librarian, Professor Charles C. Jewett, who had been in Europe purchasing books for the library, had charge of the instruction in French in my sophomore year. He was greatly beloved by the students. It was with much regret that we saw him accept the post of librarian of the Smithsonian Institution. He afterwards became the librarian of the Boston Public Library, and died at a comparatively early age.

Fortunately his place in the classroom was taken by George W. Greene, the well-known historical scholar. His life had been chiefly spent in Europe. The revolutions of 1848 were raging while we were under him. Greatly to our delight, and I may add to our profit, his time in the classroom, under the provocation of questions from us, was chiefly spent in discussing European affairs, and especially in describing the eminent persons who were conducting the military or political movements. Not a few of these he knew personally. None of us, who hung upon his lips in these hours, can ever forget his narratives. He had the

art of the best French *raconteur.* I confess
that my own intense interest in European
politics and history dates from the hours I
sat under the spell of George Greene's fine
talk. And who of our American writers
has surpassed him in a pure and flowing
English style? I am sure the inspiration of
the contact with so finished a scholar was
lost on but few of the class, even though
the demands for the details of recitation
were not very exacting.

Professor Gammell had charge of our
writing and speaking and also of the work
in history. He maintained the tradition of
pure and chaste writing which, established
under Professor Goddard, has, I am happy
to believe, never been lost at Brown. He
was most exacting in his demands upon the
writers, and no one willingly subjected himself to the humour and the stings of his
pungent criticism. Even those who could
not at the time receive them with complacency lived to recognize in them with gratitude "the wounds of a friend." No teacher
rejoiced more than he in the success of his
students in life or watched their careers
with more interest. His course in history
was fuller than that at any other college
except Harvard. It was chiefly devoted
to English constitutional history, though

some time was given to American constitutional history. It called for solid and fruitful work.

According to the custom of those days in all the colleges, one man was called to give instruction in several sciences. This man was Professor Chace. He taught chemistry, geology, botany, and physiology. At times he also conducted classes in Butler's Analogy. He really ought to have been assigned to the teaching of philosophy. His natural bent was towards metaphysics. His mind was singularly acute, his mental processes were most logical; his style of expression was absolutely lucid. His instruction was, therefore, highly appreciated, though from the brevity of the courses he could give us only elementary instruction in science. Laboratories had not then been introduced anywhere in this country. His opinion on any subject carried great weight with the students. It was generally believed that no one could outwit him by any trick or device. Therefore the vain attempt was seldom made.

Professor Caswell, who gave instruction in mathematics, astronomy, and natural philosophy, had of all the teachers the strongest hold on the affections of the students. To him every one who needed sympathy or counsel instinctively went. His great warm heart drew all to him. He had the gift of making mathematics attractive to most students, and even tolerable to that inconsiderable number who had no gift or no taste for the study. When the vote on recommending for degrees was to be taken, he looked with abundant charity on those who had never been able to pass the examinations in mathematics, saying amiably, "Let them pass. The conies are a feeble folk." The impress of his beautiful character upon all the students was never forgotten or entirely effaced.

President Wayland taught us intellectual and moral philosophy, political economy, and (in a brief course) the evidences of Christianity. I have met not a few of the men whom the world has called great; but I have seldom met a man who so impressed me with the weight of his personality as did Dr. Wayland. After making due allowance for the fact that I was but a youth when I sat under his teaching, I still think that by his power of intellect, of will, and of character, he deserved to be ranked with the strongest men our country has produced. It may be said of him as of his friend, Mark Hopkins, that his published writings do not adequately represent the

man as his pupils knew him. As a teacher
he was unsurpassed. His power of analyz-
ing a subject into its simple elements and
his power of happy illustration, often
humorous, were equally marked. One-
fourth of my classmates were Southerners.
When we came to the subject of slavery in
our study of moral philosophy, we discussed
it for three weeks. The robust personality
of Dr. Wayland was felt throughout the
whole life of the institution. The discipline
which was administered exclusively by him
was unnecessarily rigorous, the standard
of scholarship was high, the intellectual
demands upon the students were exacting.
For those who attained high rank the life
was a strenuous one. The method pursued was specially calculated to cultivate
the powers of analysis and memory. Where-
ever the subject permitted of such treatment, we were always required to begin
the recitation by giving an analysis of the
discussion in the text-book or the lecture.
We were then expected to take up point
after point of the lesson and recite without
being aided by questions from the teacher.
There was a general belief among the students, though no formal statement to that
effect was made by the Faculty, that they
would gain higher credit by repeating the

language of the book than by reporting the substance of the thought in their own language. By dint of continued memorizing, some of the students attained to a remarkable development of the verbal memory. I think that nearly one-fourth of the men in my class in their senior year used to learn in two hours — and that after an indigestible dinner in Commons — fifteen pages of Smyth's "Lectures on History," so that they could repeat them with little variation from the text. The training in analysis was of very high value in teaching men to seize and hold the main points in an argument and to make points distinctly in the construction of a discourse. On looking back, I think most of the old students will agree that too much value was attached to *memoriter* recitations.

But none the less, many of them have found great advantage in life in the facility which they acquired in retaining with accuracy what they read or write. The reaction against training the memory has probably gone too far in these later days. The natural sciences were taught as skilfully as they well could be in an overcrowded curriculum, and in days when laboratory methods were not employed. Personally I gained great advantage by being permitted to assist the

Professor of Chemistry for two years in preparing the experiments which he made before the class. In the ancient languages, certainly in Greek, I think the professors who taught us would now say too much time was given to grammatical and philological detail and too little to rapid reading. But their method was then generally in vogue, and the teaching was excellent of its kind.

To nearly every student the most important event in his college life in those days was the contact with the vigorous and suggestive mind of Dr. Wayland, in the senior classroom, and especially during the study of moral philosophy. It is difficult for those who know Dr. Wayland only by his writings, valuable as some of them are, to understand how he made so deep an impression on his pupils. He was not a great scholar; he was imperious, sometimes prejudiced; but his mind was singularly penetrating and lucid. He insisted on the clearest and sharpest definition of terms before answering a question or engaging in a discussion, and thus often made the inquirer answer his own question by an accurate definition or rendered the discussion superfluous. Withal, he had the keenest wit and a thorough knowledge of men, especially of students. He had the happiest way, often a homely way, of stating an important truth so that it remained forever fixed in the mind of the hearer. There was, too, beyond all this, a certain power of personal presence, a force of character, a moral strength, which lent a tremendous weight to even his commonest words. I have met in my day not a few distinguished men; but I recall none who have so impressed me with their power of personality, none who have uttered so many wise words which I recall every week to my advantage and help in the duties of my daily life. He was a very inapt pupil who passed from under Dr. Wayland's instruction without catching something of his catholic spirit, his passionate love of soul-liberty, and his earnest Christian principle.

The following incidents will give one an idea of his manner in the classroom. One day a rather conceited man said in the class when Dr. Wayland was speaking of the great wisdom of the Proverbs in the Scriptures, "I do not think there is anything very remarkable in the Proverbs. They are rather commonplace remarks of common people." "Very well," replied the Doctor, "make one."

The Doctor's son, Heman Lincoln Wayland, one of my classmates, inherited from his father a very keen wit. The passes between father and son were often very entertaining to the class. One day when we were considering a chapter in the father's text book on Moral Philosophy, Lincoln arose with an expression of great solemnity and respect and said, "Sir, I would like to propound a question." "Well, my son, go on," was the reply. "Well, sir," said the son, "in the learned author's work which we are now perusing I observe the following remark," and then he quoted. The class saw that fun was at hand, and began to laugh. "Well, what of that?" said the father, with a merry twinkle in his eye. "Why, this," continued the son. "In another work of the same learned author, entitled 'On the Limitations of Human Responsibility,' I find the following passage.' He then quoted. Clearly the two passages were irreconcilable. The boys were delighted to see that the father was in a trap, and broke into loud laughter. The Doctor's eyes twinkled more merrily, as he asked, "Well, what of that?" "Why," said the son with the utmost gravity, "it has occurred to me that I should like to know how the learned author reconciles the two statements." "Oh," said the father, "that is simple enough. It only shows that since he wrote the first book the learned author has learned something."

And this remark reveals one of the striking characteristics of Dr. Wayland's mind. It was ever growing. It cost him no struggle to change his opinion when he had good ground for so doing. He imbued his students with this open-mindedness. He encouraged the fullest and freest discussion in the class. The passage in Milton's Areopagitica about letting truth grapple with error was often on his lips.

During the spring of my Sophomore year there arose among the students a deep interest in personal religion. Though like most school boys I had thought with some seriousness upon religious subjects, I had been repelled by the extravagances and excitements of so-called revivals in the country towns and villages, which apparently appealed to ignorant and emotional persons rather than to the rational and intelligent. But here my thoughtful and even my merry companions addressed themselves calmly but earnestly to the great question of determining their duty to God and of deciding with what aim and what spirit they should live. The high resolves then

4　　　[33]

formed shaped the careers of a good number of the most conspicuous men in college. I think they would generally testify that they were greatly aided in that critical period of their lives by the wise counsels of Dr. Caswell and Dr. Wayland. Perhaps at no other time did the latter so deeply impress the students as when, standing in the midst of them in the old chapel, and resting one foot on a seat and his arm on the raised knee, he looked into their faces with those piercing eyes and spoke with fatherly tenderness of the divine love. With what pathos he repeated the parable of the Prodigal Son. None of his published sermons gives one any adequate idea of the power of those heart-to-heart talks.

But to us country boys, as we entered upon college life, nothing was more fascinating and more novel and more helpful than the access to well-furnished libraries and the society of students of marked ability and scholarly enthusiasm. The boys who are reared in the neighbourhood of libraries can have no appreciation of the sensations which we country lads, whose supply of books had been the most meagre imaginable, but whose thirst for reading was insatiable, experienced in being ushered into a large library and told that all

these books were now at our service. I
sometimes tremble to think what an on-
slaught we made upon the crowded shelves.
Fortunately association with older students
soon helped us learn how and what to read.
For there was at that time — and, I hope,
always — in Brown a profound interest in
literary culture. The students, with few
exceptions, lodged in the dormitories, and
took their meals in Commons Hall. They
went little into society in the city. They
were thus drawn very close to each other.
The enthusiasm of the more gifted and accomplished scholars was caught in some
degree by nearly all. I remember that men
were divided as Carlyleists or anti-Carlyle-
ists, Coleridgeians or anti-Coleridgeians,
and so on, and that literary, historic, and
philosophic theories were as hotly discussed
as the current political questions of the day.
Not wishing to be unduly *laudator temporis
acti*, I am sure that whoever examines the
triennial catalogue of Brown for the years
from 1845 to 1852, will see that the college
contained within its walls in those years a
good number, perhaps an exceptionally
large number, of men whose lives have
shown that it must have been a high privilege to be intimately associated with them
in the companionship of student life. The

society of some of them has been one of the chief factors in my own education, both in college and afterward, and one of the chief delights of life. On the whole I think that any student in Brown University who did not graduate in those days with a mind well disciplined for entering upon any worthy career was himself greatly at fault.

The careers of the men who were in college in my time furnish the best proof of the value of the training then given. I may name a few of one hundred and forty students who were my college mates. In the class of 1846 were Thomas Durfee, Chief Justice of Rhode Island, a man of poetic gifts as well as of legal attainments; Franklin J. Dickman, a Justice of the Supreme Court of Ohio, a man of fine literary taste and acquirements; Samuel S. Cox, for many years a prominent member of Congress, first from Ohio, and afterwards from New York, and subsequently United States Minister to Turkey, a gifted speaker; and Francis Wayland, Dean of the Yale Law School. In the class of 1847 were Professor George P. Fisher, of the Yale Theological School, distinguished as a writer in ecclesiastical history, and James P. Boyce, President of the Southern Baptist Theological School at Louisville, Kentucky. In the class of 1848 was Pendleton Murrah, Governor of Texas in the last years of the Civil War. In my own class, 1849, were Benjamin F. Thurston, one of the leading patent lawyers in the country; James Tillinghast, long the leading lawyer in Rhode Island on real estate; Julian Hartridge, a most eloquent member of the Confederate Congress, and afterwards of the Union Congress, and Rowland Hazard, one of the most eminent business men of his time and endowed with superior scientific and literary gifts. In the class of 1850 were James O. Murray, a prominent Presbyterian divine and Professor and Dean in Princeton College, and Edward L. Pierce, conspicuous in public affairs in Massachusetts and biographer of Charles Sumner. In the class of 1851 was Professor J. L. Diman whom I regard as one of the most gifted men I have known, the most conspicuous teacher of history of his generation, but who died while in the very prime of his strength.

We students in Brown believed that there was no better teaching in any college than in ours. Since reading Senator Hoar's description of the instruction at Harvard at the same time, and Andrew D. White's description of the instruction at Yale a little later, I am inclined to think that our

[37]

impression was correct. The one college teacher of that time whose instruction took rank with that of Dr. Wayland was Mark Hopkins, President of Williams College.

Immediately after leaving college I had an experience not unusual for young graduates. It was necessary for me to do something for my maintenance; but I found nowhere any call for my services. I had left the warm and genial atmosphere of college life to plunge into the great busy world and realized what Schiller meant when he said he stretched out his arms to serve the world and found he had clasped a lump of ice. The great, busy world went on its way and apparently had no use for me and no sympathy with me. The contrast between the warm companionships of college days and this sense of loneliness and isolation and uselessness made the experience of those few weeks following graduation the most painful of my life. The recollection of it has led me often to warn students against being too much discouraged by a similar fortune.

For in due time I was invited to take the place of Assistant Librarian in Brown University for a part of each day, and to spend another part in teaching a boy who was prevented by weakness of his eyes from the study of books. The compensation was very modest, but it gave me the great delight of returning to the society of college friends and teachers, and the equal delight of having free access to the library, and, incidentally, of guiding to a considerable degree the reading of undergraduates. During the work of classifying and arranging the books in the library an amusing incident occurred, deserving perhaps to be recorded among the "Curiosities of Literature." One of the staff, coming upon Edgeworth's book on "Irish Bulls," catalogued and placed it among the works on agriculture. This was itself one of the best of Irish Bulls.

I read aloud from one to two hours a day interesting books to my pupil, and was surprised to find how many volumes we finished by reading thus for about six months.[1] I gave a part of my leisure hours

[1] I take pleasure in saying that this receptive pupil, with whom I maintained the relations of the most cordial friendship until his death, was Thomas Poynton Ives, son of Moses Brown Ives, of the house of Brown and Ives. When the Civil War broke out, young Ives placed his yacht at the service of the government, enlisted as the commander of it, equipped it for service, and was stationed in the Chesapeake. He married Miss Motley, daughter of Motley the historian, but did not long survive the marriage. She afterward married Sir William Vernon Harcourt, the distinguished English statesman.

to my classical studies, re-reading "Virgil" and reading for the first time Demosthenes' "Oration on the Crown."

In the spring of 1850 I took a severe cold, which seriously affected my throat. Never having been ill, it did not occur to me that I ought to refrain for a time from oral instruction to my pupil. I continued to talk and read five hours a day to him until I became too hoarse to continue. I thus fastened an inflammation on my throat, from which I have never fully recovered. I returned to my father's house and spent the summer in the attempt to recuperate, but was only partially successful. Meantime my classmate and intimate friend, Rowland Hazard, had been suffering from hemorrhage of the lungs. His father, Rowland G. Hazard, a prosperous manufacturer, who afterwards became somewhat noted for writings on philosophic subjects, and who in early life had travelled on business errands extensively in the South, thought that it would be beneficial to his son to make a journey on horseback through the South. But he deemed it hardly prudent for the young man to go alone. So, knowing my condition, he invited me to accompany his son on this southern journey, and I accepted the invitation with pleasure.

II

THE SOUTHERN JOURNEY

SETTING out on my southern journey, I left home October 5, 1850, and went to Peace Dale. Tuesday evening we started for Philadelphia via New York. We spent some days in Philadelphia, where my friend had numerous relatives. During our stay we heard Albert Barnes preach a very plain and simple sermon, somewhat in the style of his then famous notes on the Gospels. We also heard Jenny Lind, then on her first tour, sing. I have never been so impressed by singing as by her rendering of "I know that my Redeemer liveth." Philadelphia had many objects of interest to me, Independence Hall, the Mint, the Schuylkill, Fairmount, etc.

We got our outfit of saddles and bridles and went via Baltimore to Harper's Ferry and Winchester. When we had planned to set out on horseback for a journey through the South, we had clothed ourselves in suits of heavy gray cloth, and steeple-crowned, brick-coloured hats, known as California hats. We had india-rubber ponchos for use

in rainy weather. Our effects were packed
in saddle bags. We purchased two excellent horses here.

We had letters to some intelligent men
in Winchester. From conversation with
them we received the impression that the
more thoughtful regarded slavery as economically of no advantage to that section;
but they did not relish the attitude of the
North in criticizing them for continuing to
maintain it. Some of them seemed to be in
a rather confused state of mind, admiring
the prosperity of the North, expressing de-
votion to the Union, but defending their
course in retaining their negroes in bondage.[1]

[1] One gentleman, who had attended the annual meeting
of the Railroad Company at Harper's Ferry, and had in-
dulged rather freely in the beverages offered, amused us
by a sort of speech, with which he welcomed us. The
following are extracts:

"Gentlemen, we welcome you to Virginia. It is all
important that you go back with right impressions, that
you should go back Union men. Now my niggers live
the same as I do, not at the same table, but have the same
food. Every dish is carried for them into an adjoining
room, a *plastered* room, Gents.

"What is the use then of kicking up such a fuss in the
kitchen? Why don't we say that you sha'n't have gray
cattle or no cattle or yellow cattle? What business is that
to us? Now would it not be a pretty spectacle to see the
bayonets at Springfield clashing with those made at
Harper's Ferry? Would it not be sublime, Gents of the

[42]

We were deeply impressed with the prosperity of the Shenandoah Valley as we travelled along its great highway. Wagons laden with corn and the other products of

North, to see you and me sticking each other in the abdomen? What do you want to do it for? New England, God bless her! We love her. All the goods I sell come from New England. She is the bone and the sinew and the back and the breast and the head and the all. We love her, we do. We want you to go North with right impressions.

"Then there is a man up above here that has two hundred nappy-heads. Now, Gents, that seems strange to you. Yet they fare well. Now here's my Jim. What is the matter with him? That's Jim, sleeps eighteen hours out of the twenty-four. Gents, you can see plenty of pretty girls in Virginia, with Virginia fortunes, ten niggers, and if you want to marry one you can do it fast enough. You tell her you are an abolitionist. She kisses you a few times, says the niggers are doing well enough. Pretty soon you would fight for them niggers. It is so, Gents. Now, Gentlemen of the North, why can't we keep united? The Jews were formerly the chosen people of God. Now if you'll look in Deuteronomy, Exodus, somewhere along there, you'll find they disobeyed God and He set his face against them and turned to the Gentile nations of the West. We are the West, Gents. We are a great and growing country. We are E Pluribus Unum, One out of many. God bless us! What is the use then, I say, of kicking up a row in the kitchen? We of the South want you of the North to go back with right impressions, Union men. Amicitia, Amor, et Veritas. Love your country and be true; the translation of that is, Gents, love America and be true."

[43]

the fertile farms passed on in continuous procession towards Winchester, the terminus
of the railway from Harper's Ferry. We
visited Weyer's Cave, which though not so
extensive as the better known Mammoth
Cave in Kentucky, was as beautiful and
striking to us who had never seen such a
geological formation. From Waynesboro
we crossed the Blue Ridge by the Rockfish
Gap. Under Monsieur Crozet, a French
engineer, the men were driving the tunnel
for the railway. Our immediate destination
was Charlottesville. We wished to visit
Monticello, the home of Jefferson, and the
University of Virginia.

We reached Turpin's Hotel in the afternoon. Our costume was hardly calculated
to impress strangers with the idea that we
were entitled to special civilities at their
hands. In fact we had generally been taken
by the men we had met on the road for
drovers, who were seeking cattle, or for bill
collectors, sent out by northern firms to dun
their debtors. More than once those who
held the latter theory put whip to their
horses to escape from us.

But in the evening we had a fine example
of Virginia hospitality. In some way a
group of gentlemen sitting near us in the
hotel learned the object of our visit to the

town, and notwithstanding our costume
proffered their services to make our visit
agreeable. The oldest of them, Mr. William Gilmer, widely known as we soon
learned as Billy Gilmer, introduced himself,
saying that he had received courtesies in
New England and that he and his friends
would be glad to entertain us. He introduced us to them and immediately began to
lay out a programme of hospitalities which
would have occupied us for a week or ten
days. "You will go to dinner with me to-
night, to-morrow we will go to Southold's,
the next day we will have a fox hunt," and
so on. We were obliged to decline this
kind offer; but we told him we should be
obliged to him if he could help us gain
access to Monticello, since we had heard it
was closed to visitors. "Oh, yes," he replied, "I will go with you to-morrow
morning. As a child I grew up a neighbour
of Jefferson and was often in his house. I
will see that you get in."

The next morning he appeared at the
appointed hour. Monticello is about two
miles from the town. As we rode up the
hill he told us some interesting stories
about Mr. Jefferson, which I here give on
his authority.

The view from the hill commands the two

fertile counties of Fluvanna and Louisa. "If in the place of them there had been a lake," Jefferson used to say, "this would have been the finest situation on earth." "And," added Mr. Gilmer, "if he could have had his way, he would have sunk them both in the lake."

Pointing to a wooded peak rising behind Monticello, he said that Mr. Jefferson once planned a sawmill to be placed there and driven by a windmill, since there is always a breeze up there. When some wood-man asked how he would get the logs up there to be sawed, he was nonplussed.

Mr. Jefferson, who was much interested in scientific matters, had been led to adopt the theory that the western prairies were almost treeless because the mastodons, believed to be arboraceous, had gnawed down and consumed the trees which originally grew on them. A wag of the neighbourhood, Billy Preston, was aware of Jefferson's views on this subject. On a journey which Preston made to Illinois, he wrote to Jefferson that he had found a remarkable confirmation of his theory. He had come upon the remains of a mastodon in a slough, in which the animal had been mired, and just where the stomach must have been there was a great mass of what appeared to be sawdust, evidently the tree which had been eaten. Mr. Jefferson was so gratified at this news that he at once wrote a Memoir on the matter and sent it to his scientific correspondents in France.

We passed the monument to Jefferson just before we reached the entrance to the grounds. It was badly mutilated by visitors who had broken off chips of the stone as souvenirs. The steward in charge of the estate happened to be near the gate which, however, was locked. Mr. Gilmer shouted to him from afar in the most familiar manner; but as we reached the gate, the steward informed us that Captain Levy, the naval officer, into whose possession the estate had come through his marriage, had left the strictest orders that during his absence in Europe no one should be admitted to the house. We had heard that Captain Levy had taken offence because he had not been received as *persona grata* by his neighbours. On the announcement by the steward of this prohibition, Mr. Gilmer evinced deep anguish. "This is really too bad," he exclaimed. "Here are two sons of ,old acquaintances and friends of Mr. Jefferson, who have ridden hundreds of miles to pay a tribute to his memory, to visit his residence as a sacred shrine, and now they

are to be shut out. If Mr. Jefferson were
alive, how he would have greeted them!
Oh no! this cannot be, my good friend.
Allow me, sir, to introduce you to Mr.
Charles Francis Adams, the son of John
Quincy Adams, and to Mr. Fletcher Webster, the son of Daniel Webster!" As it
happened he called me, who was about the
size of Mr. Adams, Mr. Webster, and Mr.
Hazard, who was six feet high, Mr. Adams.
He had not notified us of his intention to
play this trick, and it required our best
efforts to play the parts assigned us without breaking into laughter. The steward
was evidently a little puzzled to explain to
himself how so distinguished men should
appear in such costume. But he yielded
to Mr. Gilmer's request with the remark
that he supposed Captain Levy would not
object to the admission of such visitors.
We were shown about the grounds and the
house. In Jefferson's sleeping room was
the bed on which he died, July 4, 1826.
On the mantel were two small statues of
him. In the dining room was a bust of
Voltaire. The furniture of the house was
wrapped in coverings. In the silence and
the dim light which was admitted through
the half-closed shutters, the house in which
so many statesmen had discussed the grav-

est public questions seemed in fact a tomb. For once even the merry talk of our friend Gilmer fell with a certain dissonance on the ear.

In the afternoon we rode out to the University. A student, Mr. Chalmers, introduced us to the Librarian, Mr. Wirtenbaker, who received us very cordially. The student's dormitories and the lecture halls, planned as was the University itself by Mr. Jefferson, still stand as we saw them on two sides of the beautiful Green, though other and finer structures have since been added.

Perhaps this is the best place to say that I attended the inauguration of President Alderman, in the spring of 1905. Being invited to speak at the banquet, I found that there were few, if any, persons present whose memory of the town and the University reached back as far as mine. When I gave some of the reminiscences above recorded, the audience seemed highly entertained, especially by my report of the acts and stories of "Billy Gilmer," the reputation of whose wit and humour has survived in that region.

We crossed the Blue Ridge to Staunton. On this journey we first saw negro women working in the fields. In Staunton we

5 [49]

visited the State Institution for the Blind
and for the Deaf and Dumb, and the State
Lunatic Asylum. From Staunton we went
to Lexington, then and afterwards noted
for the State Military Institute, at which
some of the most distinguished confederate
officers were educated. Stonewall Jackson
was a professor here when the Civil War
broke out.

My journey up the Shenandoah Valley
proved of essential service to me in my
editorial work during the war, because
that valley was the scene of so many military operations of importance, which I had
occasion to discuss.

From Lexington we went to the Natural
Bridge, where the boldness of the scenery
surpassed our expectations. We started
from the bridge for the Balcony Falls on
the James River. On our journey, when we
supposed we must be approaching our destination, we inquired of a man whom we
met how far it was to Balcony Falls. He
looked at us in astonishment. He said he
had never heard of them. We expressed
our surprise at this, when suddenly he put
his hand to his forehead and exclaimed,
"Oh, you mean Bel-cō-ny (with the accent
on the second syllable) Falls," and then gave
us the desired information. We found

[50]

them, a picturesque spot, where the river
breaks through a narrow gorge filled with
rocks. Passing a tollgate on our ride, we
asked the gatekeeper, a woman, how much
we had to pay for two of us. She replied
that the toll was three cents for one, but
she was unable to reckon the total amount
for two. As my companion was noted in
college for his mathematical attainments, I
called on him to solve the problem, which
he did, and we passed through.

By almost impassable roads and lanes we
went to the Peaks of Otter. We forded one
stream thirty-two times in going seven
miles. The views from these peaks were
very extensive and impressive. None, we
were assured, on all the mountain ranges of
Virginia are more so. We paused a few
hours in Lynchburg, which then had about
eight hundred inhabitants. Its chief trade
was in tobacco. We went next to Danville. On the way we passed the Isle of
Pines, lying in Staunton River, and formerly
owned by Patrick Henry. We also passed
two small villages known by the significant
names of Hard Times and Scuffletown. We
were told by one of the natives that in that
region they raised "a right smart chance of
sheep and snorting crops of tobacco." But
the soil was really thin and in a large part

of our route covered with forest. We met hardly any travellers in a whole day's ride. So far as we could judge from our conversations with Virginians on our whole journey from Winchester to Danville, that is from Northern to Southern Virginia, opinions as to the desirableness of maintaining slavery were divided. Not a few were convinced that it was of no advantage to their State. But no one could make the journey we did without being impressed with the great natural resources of the State, with the attractiveness of the scenery on both sides of the Blue Ridge, and with the shrewdness, intelligence, and activity of the inhabitants of the Shenandoah Valley.

Passing from Danville into North Carolina, we travelled on a level ridge for twenty-seven miles without crossing a stream. We came also on the first camp we had seen of a slave trader, buying up negroes to take to the gulf states. That was a prosperous business both in Virginia and in the Carolinas. Some of the table arrangements in Danville and in towns further south were novel. Beef steak was served in a large, deep potato dish, from which you drew your rations with a spoon. Butter, a most liberal supply, from one to three pounds,

was placed in slices on the largest plate on
the table. Sometimes this plate was placed
on an inverted bowl, sometimes on a cir-
cular board twelve or fifteen inches in di-
ameter, which was supported on a wooden
standard a foot high.

Our journey to Greensboro, North Carolina (named after General Green of revolutionary fame), took us over the battlefield
of Guilford Court House, and over the region
in which Cornwallis and Green contended
for some time. A venerable man, said to be
the oldest in Martinsville, assured us that
Washington fought the battle with Cornwallis and won it. He modestly added that
he remembered nothing more about it.

Near Greensboro we visited the Hodgins
Gold Mine, which was then worked with
profit, but like the other North Carolina
gold mines was afterwards abandoned.
The gold was found chiefly in the earthy
matter which surrounded the loose quartz.
Copper was also found. We also went to
see the mines of Gold Hill where they were
taking out four hundred dollars worth of
gold daily.

We passed through Salisbury to Char-
lotte. There was here a branch mint,
where they made no coins larger than five
dollar pieces. They employed only four

men in their work. We crossed the State line into South Carolina, and traversed Lancaster County, passing over the scene of Sumter's and of Gates' military operations in the Revolution. The soil was light and sandy. Lofty pines were here first encountered. In this region we met the first advocates of secession. Some of them warned us that it would be dangerous for us to approach Columbia. We replied that we would continue our journey until we saw signs of danger.

Camden we found an attractive town of between two and three thousand inhabitants. De Kalb's remains lie beneath a monument in the Presbyterian church. His name was given to a cotton factory which we visited. Near it was the figure of an iron man on which Colonel Dickinson, killed in the Mexican War, had practised with his pistol in preparation for a duel. We were told that a duel had been fought in the town a year before our visit, and another two years before. Public opinion seemed to approve of duelling. Camden was Cornwallis' headquarters at one period in his southern campaign. The Camden *Journal* was a violent secession sheet.

On the road from Camden to Columbia we passed large fields of cotton, one a mile long. As the Legislature was in session we found it impossible to gain admission to any hotel, but after a long search in the evening were received at a boarding house. The next day being Sunday, we had the good fortune to hear Rev. Dr. Thornwell, one of the most distinguished preachers in the South, deliver the baccalaureate sermon to the graduating class of the University of South Carolina. It was a discourse of great power.

On the next day we attended the Commencement exercises. The Governor (Seabrook), the President of the Senate, the Speaker of the House, and a group of prominent citizens occupied the stage. We were rather surprised to see a supply of cuspidors on the stage for tobacco chewers, and they were by no means superfluous furniture. We thought the students' speeches were only moderately good. The President's address to them was solely an appeal to them to abide by the State in the dissolution of the Union which he regarded as inevitable. He exhorted them to fight and conquer or fall beneath the Palmetto banner. Several of the students' speeches referred to the secession of the States as certain to come.

On the following day we visited the Legislature. The halls were hung in mourning for Calhoun. During this session the speeches abounded with allusions to the coming dissolution of the Union. In the evening we took tea with Mrs. McCord, a most gifted and learned woman, the daughter of that eminent statesman, Langdon Cheves. Though extremely cordial to us personally, she expressed what seemed to be the general feeling in Columbia when she said to us, "We ought to fight you of the North." It will be remembered that this was nearly nine years before the attack on Fort Sumter.

From Columbia we set out for Augusta, Georgia. At the end of the second day's journey we halted before a house and inquired for Leestown, which appeared on the map. No other house was visible. "This is Leestown," responded a man, who proved to be Mr. Lee. He informed us — we had not failed to observe it — that the land in that neighbourhood produced little or nothing. The country we had passed through was of course very sparsely settled. We lodged at Mr. Lee's. As we entered Hamburg, opposite Augusta, we saw twenty negroes marching round a piazza singing merrily. They were for sale. Not even this fact depressed their spirits.

We found Augusta the most attractive

southern city we had seen. It had about twelve thousand inhabitants. The two principal streets were lined with fine dwellings. One of them, a mile or more in length, had two rows of trees in the middle, and one row on each side. There were two large cotton mills under the charge of a man brought from Lowell, Massachusetts. They were as well equipped as any we had seen at home. The operatives were all white. We made a vain attempt to sell our horses, as we learned that owing to the sparseness of the population in southwestern Georgia we should find it very uncomfortable travelling on horseback to middle Florida, where we had decided to go for the remainder of the winter. We left the horses in Augusta, while we went by rail to Charleston, South Carolina.

We had to leave at five A.M., without breakfast. We stopped for breakfast near Aiken. Mr. Hazard paid for our meals. As we were sitting by the fire near a Virginian, the whistle blew and we three started for the train. A negro waiter came running after us, exclaiming, "Didn't one of you gemmens forget to pay for breakfast?" Mr. Hazard replied, "We paid." The Virginian, looking the negro fiercely in the eye, said sharply, "Which is it? Point

him out." "I d'n know," said the negro.
"Point him out," repeated the Virginian.
By this time the cars were moving and we
all jumped in. "That is my fix," coolly
remarked the Virginian to us.

Till we were within four miles of Charleston, we were passing through a succession
of cypress swamps and pine barrens. We
spent a few days in Charleston most agree-
ably. Our classmate, Mendenhall, and
friends to whom we had letters, received us
with the hospitality characteristic of that
city. The houses were generally built in
the Grecian style of architecture, with
broad piazzas on three sides. Magnolias
and live oaks abounded in the open spaces.
We made an excursion up Cooper's River
to see the rice fields, and to Sullivan's
Island, which was then a summer resort
for the Charlestonians. We obtained our
trunks which we had sent by sea from
Baltimore. Mr. Hazard had been robbed
of a part of his wardrobe; but we were
enabled to lay aside our suits of Vermont
gray and dress in proper form to receive
the hospitalities of our friends.

Mr. and Mrs. McCord having invited us
when we were at Columbia to spend the
Christmas holidays with them on their
plantation at Fort Motte, some thirty miles

south of Columbia, we gladly availed ourselves of the opportunity to see something
of plantation life under so auspicious circumstances. On December nineteenth we
went by rail from Charleston. We were
most cordially received by our host and
hostess who were living in a fine mansion
surrounded by grounds laid out in excellent
taste.

We walked out with Mr. McCord to the
negro quarters. He had one hundred and
thirty-seven negroes, and was building new
and comfortable tenements for them. He
had a house in which all the negro children
were kept during the day in charge of at-
tendants, and a hospital provided with
nurses. Every negro had his particular
task and drew his ration of food. The
arrangements were very systematical. The
children sang hymns for us and all of them
down to the veriest tot sang *con amore,* as
legs, arms, and bodies were all called into
requisition. The plantation called "Lang
Syne" had about three thousand acres and
produced from one hundred and eighty to
two hundred bales of cotton. We were
hospitably entertained by dinner parties
and hunting parties on the plantations in
the neighbourhood. Partridges, rabbits,
and squirrels were the game sought. The

negroes running and shouting rivalled the dogs in securing the game shot.

Our visit corrected our impression that the life of the planter and his wife was one free from care. They did have more leisure than the northern farmer. But careful management was required to secure good profits. And the negroes, careless about their health, called for much attention. Our hostess, during our visit, was up all night caring for a sick negro baby. She had made a careful study of political economy and had translated a valuable French work on that subject. She had given much attention to the economics of plantation life. She told us that she would prefer to have $25,000 in good bank stock rather than $100,000 in negroes and plantations. The negroes of "Lang Syne" seemed cheerful and merry, especially when they came on Christmas day to the house to draw their extra Christmas rations. But we were much impressed by an incident which occurred while, on our departure, we were on the way to the railway station. The negro driver was a grave elderly man, a Baptist preacher, in fact, for his people. I ventured to say to him, "You servants must all be very happy in your lot with such a kind master and mistress." He answered not a word, but looked at me with a surprised and pathetic air, which seemed to me to say, "You, who are from the North, ought to know that slavery is not a happy condition." I dropped the conversation, but I have never forgotten the expression of his countenance.

While waiting for a delayed train at the station, we met a hotel keeper from Quincy, Florida, whose commendations of his town decided us to go there for the winter. Mr. Hazard stopped at Aiken, where we were to remain a few days, and I went on to Augusta to bring the horses down. The people at the hotel hardly recognized me, as I no longer wore the riding costume in which they had seen me. The horses having been in the stable three weeks I had a lively time, riding one and leading the other. It rained heavily all day. I arrived at Aiken soaked to the skin. The next day as Mr. Hazard and I were taking a ride, his horse ran away and he was thrown heavily against a tree, but fortunately my fear that he was seriously hurt proved to be unfounded. We sold the horses and saddles and bridles for a little more than they cost us. We remained a week in Aiken. It rained almost every day, and once we had snow three or four inches deep at which some of the negro children were much excited, as they had never before seen it.

On January 6, 1851, we set out from Aiken for Florida. We sat up, as there were no sleeping cars on the trains in those days, all night on the journey from Augusta to Atlanta. This place was just getting started as the junction point of three railroads. We went on at once to Macon, the farthest point on our route which we could then reach by rail. At 10.30 P.M. we started from there in a small coach. Why I know not, but all through the South the coaches which we took generally started in the night, some of them at 2 A.M. We had hardly left the town when the coach was upset, and unluckily the only door was on the side next to the ground. We broke the window on the other side and crawled out into the mud. I took the driver's lantern and walked ahead, while Mr. Hazard held up the coach to keep it from capsizing again. After awhile we remounted, but had not gone far before the coach fell plump into a mud hole so as to pitch off a clergyman from the driver's seat and to pitch the driver off headlong after him. It proved we were near a camp of negro teamsters who had a lightwood fire and

some loads of furniture. We cut down
chairs and sat by the fire and waited until nearly daylight, when a larger and better coach came to our relief. Frequently,
during the journey the mud was so deep
that we had to alight and walk in the
night as well as in the daytime to enable
the horses to draw the empty vehicle. As
I sat with the driver, he pointed out to me
the sloughs in which the coach had been
upset on previous trips. The food at the
inns was as bad as could be.

One day we had a long fast because we
reached no inn. The country was very
sparsely settled. The roads were indescrib-
ably bad; swamps, corduroys, roots of trees,
gullies, mud holes, creeks to be forded, were
our obstacles. Three nights we travelled
in these conditions, much of the time in
heavy rain, and finally reached Quincy at
2 A.M., after the most fatiguing and uncomfortable journey we had ever taken.
This was Friday morning and we had not
been in bed since Sunday night. Southwestern Georgia, as we saw it, was not
very inviting.

As we were taking a late breakfast in the
hotel, the morning of our arrival, we witnessed a scene which was disturbing to
northern young men. The negro waiter

[63]

whom we had sent to the kitchen to fill our order, in crossing the back yard, fell into a fight with another negro. In the midst of the tumult a white man appeared with a raw hide and began to lay it on the back of our waiter with great force. The boy in his pain ran and struck his head repeatedly against the brick wall as if to dash out his brains. But the white man continued his blows until the negro fell to the ground. We were told that the white man was his owner and was a citizen of New Jersey, of a family so distinguished that if I should mention his name most readers of these lines would recall it as familiar. It is needless to say that we did not care for any more breakfast.

We walked out soon after to the front of the courthouse, where a crowd was gathered. We found they were selling at auction the slaves of a citizen who had recently died. The negro families that were to be separated were evincing much feeling. A fine looking girl, about eighteen years old, was mounting the block as we arrived. The auctioneer rudely proceeded to speak of her good points, as he might of those of a horse. He made her show her teeth, coarse men came to feel of her ankles and the calves of her legs, to test the quality of her muscles. It was the most repulsive and disgusting spectacle we had ever seen. We felt that this scene and that at the hotel were showing us a side of slavery that we had learned nothing of in the hospitable homes of South Carolina. Near the town there were constantly camps of negroes, whom slave dealers had brought from the northern slave states.

We spent three months in Quincy. A considerable company of invalids were wintering there. As we met each morning at the post-office, their habitual conversation concerning their coughs and expectorations and other tuberculous symptoms, were not very exhilarating, though fortunately we were not ill enough to be much disturbed by them. We were very hospitably received by the citizens, many of whom were persons of intelligence and excellent character. That part of Florida had been mainly settled from the Carolinas. Not a few of the men, after unsuccessful business ventures elsewhere, had come there to make a fresh start in life, and were as devoted to money-getting as they supposed the Yankees to be. Land was cheap and well adapted to the growth of cotton, which was the chief crop. As no railways had reached that section, marketing the cotton

[65]

R

was difficult and costly. It was sent for shipment to St. Marks. There were in the neighbourhood an undesirable number of men who had fled from creditors with no intention of paying their debts and of men who had committed crimes in their old homes. Among this rougher element, drunkenness and violence were not uncommon. The rooms we rented were over a surgeon's office. It was a rare week when some one who had been wounded in a fray did not require the surgeon's attention. On the other hand the town was an educational centre for Middle Florida. There was an excellent boarding school for girls, kept by two cultivated women from Connecticut. There was also a boarding school for boys. The churches had one undesirable feature in their construction. They had no underpinning, but rested on posts three or four feet high. Unhappily the swine which were allowed to run in the streets made their lounging place under the churches. The rain flowed into the excavation they made, and in these pools fleas were bred in profusion. Unhappily also the floors of some of the churches were so loosely laid that the fleas often made their way up through the cracks, and climbing up under the garments of the worshippers greatly interfered with a reverential enjoyment of the services.

We thought that there and generally in the South a larger proportion of the people attended church than in the North. I have been struck with the fact that Southern political orators indulge much more than Northern speakers in scriptural allusions and quotations. Is it because the Southerners are more familiar with the Bible than the Northerners? I will mention one incident which may show that some of the southern children are as unfamiliar with it as the Northern children, whose unfamiliarity with it is so often commented on in our days. Finding that the daughter of our boarding-house keeper and some of her companions, girls of fourteen or fifteen years of age, were not much interested in the Biblical narratives, I imitated a device, which I had somewhere read about, that Franklin tried with a company of French infidels with success. Having promised to tell them an Oriental story which I thought would interest them, I narrated in my own language the story of Esther. Not one of them, it proved, had read it. When they expressed their delight with it, I told them where they would find it told in a more much touching manner.

I must repeat one incident illustrating how one's native place is to him the centre of the world. A rather dull, overgrown boy of fifteen once asked me where we came from. I replied "from Rhode Island." "How far away is that?" he asked. "About thirteen hundred miles," said I. "Golly," he rejoined, "I don't see how you stand it to live so fur off." In fact the knowledge of the life and industries and ideas of the North among even the more intelligent was naturally very limited. But they were charitable enough to me to urge me very strongly to remain in Quincy and teach.

In March we made an excursion to Tallahassee and St. Marks. The road to the capitol lay through forests and swamps. At one point near Ocklocknee Channel, posts were set up to guide the stage driver in swimming his horses where water overflowed the road. Tallahassee was made attractive by its beautiful gardens. On coming south we were impressed by the fact that the farther south we came the more intensely Calvinistic and severe was the theology which inspired the preaching. In Tallahassee we heard by far the sternest and most sulphurous discourse we listened to.

A dilapidated railway, on which a car was drawn by horses, connected the city with Newport. The one public building in this new town was used for a church, an academy, a masonic lodge, a courthouse, and a jail. From Newport we walked three miles to St. Mark's, the old seaport for this region. One warehouse and half-a-dozen dilapidated, weather-beaten houses composed the town. The remains of the old Spanish fort showed still a part of the wall and parapets and moat. General Jackson seized it in 1818. Creepers and peach trees were growing from its sides. We sailed down to the lighthouse, eight miles, passing Port Leon on the way, and gained our first view of the blue waters of the Gulf of Mexico. Here, too, we first saw cormorants and alligators. When returning by the railway we found that fire in the forests had set the track on fire at several points; but the driver put whip to his horses and carried our street car safely through the fire.

The next day we drove sixteen miles to see the Wakulla Spring. We passed a few cabins on the road, tenanted by sallow, wretched-looking people. This spring, of which the Indian name Wakulla is said to mean "Mystery," breaks out of a submerged limestone cliff, one hundred and ninety feet down and forms a pool one hun-

[69]

dred feet wide. The water is so clear that one can see a button dropped to the bottom. At certain angles one sees beautiful prismatic hues. The shadow of your boat is plainly perceptible on the bottom. You seem to be floating in the air. Near by were some of the bones of a mastodon which had been taken from the spring. The remainder of the skeleton had been sent to Barnum's Museum.

On April 2 we bade adieu to our good friends of Quincy, not one of whom have I ever seen since. We drove to Chattahoochee over a dreadful road, and in the evening took the steamer Palmetto for Columbus, where we arrived the next day at 1 P.M. The river with its precipitous banks largely covered with cypresses was of more interest than we had expected. Columbus was a prosperous city of six thousand inhabitants. Several cotton mills were in process of construction.

The next morning at 2 A.M., the usual hour in the South for stages to start, we set out for Opelika. Hardly had we seated ourselves when one of the two women passengers said to the other, "Wall, Poll, I s'pose we might as well begin to rub snuff. You got your bottle." Poll produced it and they began this disgusting habit of rubbing a little wooden swab dipped in snuff in their mouths. The odor of the smoke of the lamps and a fresh wind furnished us some relief. I may as well say in this connection that in Florida the young women of good breeding were often addicted to this habit, though in private. On this journey we met with a remarkable negro. He had purchased his freedom. He was on his way to release from arrest for drunkenness his former owner to whom he had frequently shown this kindness. He was the builder of a very long bridge which we crossed. We were told that when the builders of the capitol at Montgomery were puzzled in framing the dome, he was called in to extricate them from their trouble.

From Opelika we went seventy miles by rail to Montgomery. The view from the Capitol to the north extended over an interminable forest, clothed in the delicate green of early spring. The city lies in a semi-circle of hills, and appeared to be fairly prosperous. As we were passing some negroes, one asked, "How's de peoples up de country?" "Oh, dey's all extant," replied another. We gathered from conversation that the sentiment in Montgomery and the adjacent country was by no means unanimous for secession, though the subject was under discussion.

We proceeded by steamer to Mobile, a sail of a day and a half, through rather tame and monotonous scenery. As we passed the steamboats at the wharves in Mobile, one of our negro men would lead off in a song and the negroes on the other boats would join in a chorus. This made an animated scene of our arrival. We spent a happy day with some good friends, but were obliged to hurry on to New Orleans. The business, mainly in cotton, of Mobile had been declining, but they hoped that the completion of the Mobile & Ohio Railroad would revive it. The harbour was so shallow that much of the cotton for export had to be carried thirty miles in lighters.

We went by steamer to New Orleans. At that time, steamers and sailing ships, foreign and American, crowded the levee for miles. The products of the Mississippi Valley lay piled in confusion as far as the eye could see. Thousands of negroes were busy loading drays and ships, singing as they toiled. No other such scene could be witnessed in America. The visit to the foreign quarters, the mingling of French and Spanish with the English, the cemeteries

with their peculiar tombs, the thousand
sights which characterize a European city,
were all strange and fascinating to us.
Visiting the steamer Peytona to bid farewell to some friends, we had our first and
only view of Henry Clay who was depart-
ing for home on that boat. As was the
custom, a concourse of ladies were kissing
him good-bye. That proved, I think, to be
his last visit to New Orleans. We dined
with Jacob Barker, the most distinguished
merchant in the city, who once won a
famous law-suit, which turned on the con-
tention raised by him that a whale is not a
fish but a mammal.

On ascending the river we passed two or
three large crevasses through which the
water, pouring like a river, had flooded the
country as far as we could see, and to the
depth of several feet. The people had fled
from their houses in boats. We stopped at
Baton Rouge long enough to visit the capitol, not quite completed, and the state
prison, whose inmates were employed in a
cotton mill established within the walls.
We continued on the steamer we took at
Baton Rouge until we reached Paducah.
There we heard a Judge charging the jury
in a very original manner. He always referred to the Court as "She," and inveighed

against demagogues "honeyfogling the people."

We went by steamer to Nashville. We found the views of the bluffs on the river in refreshing contrast to the low, level, and monotonous banks of the Mississippi. The city has a fine site in the hills overlooking the Cumberland River. State prisoners were erecting the Capitol. They had been at work on it six years, and it was supposed that three years more would be required to complete it.

From Nashville we went by stage coach to the Mammoth Cave. We spent two days in exploring that most famous of all caves. A tedious stage coach journey took us from the Cave to Louisville. After a brief visit with friends, one of them our college classmate, Reuben T. Durrett, since well known as a scholar, learned in the history of Kentucky, we took the steamer for Cincinnati.

We spent Sunday in that city. By chance we went to the church of which Dr. Willis Lord, once pastor of my own church in Providence, was the pastor and heard an excellent sermon from him. On climbing the hill back of the city, we gained a view of Professor Mitchell's Observatory, of which years afterwards I heard him speak so frequently. He used to relate with pride, that in a hundred days from his departure for Europe he returned with his telescope. Few astronomers could tell in so eloquent language as he did of the revelations made to him by his instrument.

We left Cincinnati by coach at 4 o'clock A.M. for Dublin, Indiana, to visit the Vanuxems, Quaker relatives of Mr. Hazard. This drive took us through a most fertile country, inhabited by an industrious and thrifty people. When I saw a white man actually sawing his own wood, I felt like going to shake hands with him. We had come to a land where honest physical toil was honourable. The beautiful beech and maple groves of eastern Indiana, having no undergrowth, were charming to our eyes. We spent a week most pleasantly with the simple, hospitable, prosperous people of Dublin and Cambridge, and returned to Cincinnati in a long day's drive to take the steamer for Pittsburg.

No scenery we had beheld was so enchanting as that on the voyage up the Ohio. We looked up our friends, the Randolphs and Tanners, and passed a pleasant day with them. We made the journey to Johnstown by canal boat, a most agreeable mode of travelling through the romantic

[75]

valleys. At Johnstown we were drawn up an inclined plane and started by rail for Philadelphia. We called upon our old friends. I left Mr. Hazard there and reached home on May 22, after an absence of seven months and eighteen days, reinvigorated in health.

III.

WORK IN CIVIL ENGINEERING AND STUDY IN EUROPE

THE trouble with my throat described on page 40, really changed the whole plan of my life, as I had then marked it out. I had formed the purpose of studying for the ministry. Some of my most intimate college friends were already pursuing theological studies in the Andover Theological Seminary, where I used to visit them. I had formed the acquaintance of the eminent Professors, Park, Edwards, and Phelps. I had even gone so far as to engage my room for the autumn. But the trouble with my throat continued for weeks so obstinate that I deemed it wise to consult a noted Boston specialist on diseases of the throat. He informed me that I must not indulge in the hope of being able to pursue any profession in which I should have to speak in public. He said it would not be prudent for me even to attempt to teach. He advised me to choose some out-door employment. This announcement was a bitter disappointment. It seemed for a time that

[77]

every door to a career in which I had any interest was shut in my face.

I asked myself what out-of-door employment is there in which I can profit by the education I have had. I decided that civil engineering gave the best promise of fulfilling that condition. Fortunately some of my friends knew Mr. E. S. Chesboro, a former resident of Providence, and then City Engineer of Boston. In answer to their inquiries he expressed a willingness to take me into his office. I reported to him for duty in August, 1851. The work on the Cochituate water supply in Boston was not then completed, and I was employed mainly on that. In those days few men in the engineering offices had received a technical or even a mathematical education in the schools. They had usually worked their way up from the position of rodman, and they accomplished what they did by rule-of-thumb work or by the mechanical use of formulae the *rationale* or origin of which they did not know. It proved that I was the only one in the office from the chief down who had studied the Calculus, and as a real knowledge of some of the formulae for water problems involved that study, I presently found them turned over to me. As one recalls how slender were the opportunities in those days for training in engineering studies and observes the large number of excellent engineering schools in our country, one may say that in no branch of education has there been more rapid and helpful development than in that of engineering in all its applications.

The Grand Trunk road from Montreal to Boston was opened while I was in the office. I assisted in making an immense map, which was stretched in the tent on the Common when the celebration of this event was held. Lord Elgin, the Governor-general of Canada, and President Fillmore were present. I remember that as Mr. Fillmore was said to be unaccustomed to riding, I saw two negroes holding his horse carefully by the bits as the animal slowly walked in the procession. We all agreed that he was a very handsome man, but not much of a cavalier.

At one time complaint was made of the impurity of the Cochituate water in Boston. Mr. Chesboro invited me to walk with him through about two miles of the conduit, from which the water had been partially drawn off, somewhere west of Cambridge. And there on this subterranean excursion I made the acquaintance of Professor Horsford of Harvard, whose friendship I afterwards enjoyed through his life. The walking on the bottom of an egg-shaped conduit in which about a foot of water had been left was not altogether easy or agreeable. It was decided that some vegetable deposit had found its way into the water.

One day near the end of November, Mr. Chesboro assigned to me the task of making a survey and a map of Boston Common, showing every path and every tree on it. This was to be made at the request of some dweller on Beacon Street, who for many years had daily walked around the Common. I began in the corner just in front of the State House. While I was at work I received a letter from my friend Hazard saying that he was still having trouble with his lungs and that his father had decided to send him to Southern Europe for the winter and wished me to accompany him. He begged me to come to his home immediately and confer with him. I did so, and it was decided that we should sail at once. I went back to Boston, and took my leave of Mr. Chesboro, to whose kindness I was greatly indebted. So ended my work in engineering. After a brief visit to my parents, I joined Mr. Hazard and we sailed from New York for Havre on the steamship Arago, Captain Lines, on December 13.

We had only thirteen passengers. Among them were Mr. Spence of Baltimore, afterwards our Minister to Turkey, George W. Kendall, editor of the New Orleans Picayune, who greatly enlivened our voyage by his wit, and one typical specimen of the self-reliant Connecticut Yankee. This last was on his wedding trip. His opportunities for education had been limited. But he was daunted by no obstacles of travel in foreign parts. By some means he had persuaded himself that although he knew no French, he could make a French word out of an English word if he pronounced it very loudly and added the termination *bus*. So he would accost one of the waiters who were all French, thus: "Garçon, bring me some *cheese*-ibus." And in fact he generally got it. He travelled at such a pace that by the time we reached Florence he had been all through the East and was on his way home. We met him in the street in Florence one morning with one-half of his face covered with lather and inquired of him what had happened to him. With much vehemence he said: "I wanted to be shaved. I went into a shop which had a barber's pole in front and sat down. The barber soon gave me to understand that he bled people, but did not shave them. So I went to another

[81]

shop. The barber there lathered my face and began to shave me with a razor so dull that I snatched it from his hand and told him I could make a razor sharper than that on the sole of my boot. So here I am looking for another barber." We asked him how he had contrived to get all over southern and eastern Europe so rapidly and with no language but English. Holding his purse in one hand and his cane in the other, he replied, "With that purse in one hand and that cane in the other, and with swearing a little at times, I can go all over Europe." And I have reason to think he did.

We arrived at Havre on December 27. When the pilot came aboard he astonished us by the announcement that by a *coup d'état* Louis Napoleon had taken full possession of the government, that many of the prominent statesmen were in prison, and that martial law was declared. On landing, Mr. Hazard and I proceeded at once to Rouen, where we spent a day in visiting the churches. We were delighted with our first view of the florid Gothic architecture. Thence we went immediately to Paris, where we found much excitement over the *coup d'état*. The marks of the bullets which had been fired in the conflicts along the Boulevard des Italiens were still fresh.

But the places of amusement were all open. At the Theatre Français we saw that great actor Got in Molière's Malade Imaginaire and Rachel in Phèdre and the theatre was crowded on both nights. When I was in college we were, like students in most New England colleges, forbidden to attend the theatre on pain of expulsion. Therefore I had never before seen plays presented by great actors and actresses. Although my understanding of the language was imperfect, these performances were the revelation of a new world to me.[1]

We were assured that many prominent men had been thrown into prison. But so far as we could observe, business seemed to be going on everywhere, and we were not interfered with at all.

There was a notable service in Notre Dame which we attended, in which the Archbishop of Paris invoked the divine blessing on the President in his new undertaking.

We also attended a reception given by

[1] I may properly remark here that during this visit to Europe, I did not keep a diary, but wrote home my detailed letters, which were preserved until they were burned when my father's house was destroyed by fire. I depend on my present recollections for what I now write concerning the European journey.

our Consul, Mr. Goodrich, the Peter Parley, whose books have been the delight of our childhood. He appeared to us to be the impersonation of the amiable, entertaining, child-loving Peter Parley, of whom we had been so fond, and he seemed much pleased at our acknowledgment of our great indebtedness to his books.

The weather was very damp and chilly, and therefore, a week after our arrival, we set out for Marseilles on our way to Italy. Having engaged our seats in the diligence, we went to the office at the appointed hour and occupied them. The diligence was driven to the railway station and there the body was lifted with passengers and baggage by a crane and deposited on a flat car. So we were transported to Dijon, where the diligence body was again lifted by a crane and placed on wheels. We were then drawn by horses to Lyons. Thence we were taken by rail to Marseilles. On our journey we saw many citizens tied to ropes and marching under military guard to prison. Everywhere there was manifest a feeling of high tension.

A young lieutenant in uniform journeyed with us from Lyons to Marseilles. On arrival there a customs officer came to examine our baggage. The lieutenant refused to allow the officer to touch his portmanteau. When the officer insisted, the lieutenant drew his pistol and forced a retreat. After the officer left, the lieutenant turned to us with a laugh and said, "The pistol was not loaded." *Leges silent inter arma.*

From Marseilles we went by diligence via Draguignan to Genoa, and thence by sea to Naples. We spent a few days there, of course visiting Pompeii and ascending Vesuvius. We met our old teacher, Professor Gammell, who was on his wedding trip with his wife, the daughter of Robert H. Ives. He proposed to us to join them in the journey to Rome in a private carriage. In those days of few railways this was a charming method of travel. The *vetturino,* usually a Swiss, furnished the carriage and horses, stopped wherever one wished on the journey, paid all the hotel bills, and spared one all the trouble of bargaining with the natives. As there was a railway as far as Capua, Mr. Hazard and I went ahead to visit that place of so much historic interest. We drove out towards evening to the village near which Hannibal was said to have encamped, and found a most interesting fête going on. The peasants in their picturesque costumes were dancing on the

green.   On our return to the hotel we were
told that we were fortunate in escaping
robbery, since that village was the resort
at such times of some desperate characters.

Mr. and Mrs. Gammell joined us on the
next day, and we had a delightful three
days' journey to Rome.   The approach to
the city from that side is far more picturesque than from Civitavecchia or from
Florence.   We spent six weeks in the highest enjoyment I ever experienced in all my
travels.   Fresh from our college studies,
with Horace in the pocket as a guide-book,
every step revealed to us some object of the
deepest interest.   At night we returned to
our rooms to read afresh of all we had seen.
Almost literally we could say that we
travelled and observed all day and then
studied all night.   Such delights could
hardly come to one later in life.   Subsequent visits to Rome never yielded a full
repetition of the first experiences.   Rome
was also more interesting then to the young
American traveller than it is now because
it was completely under ecclesiastical control, and the streets were always gay with
processions, celebrations, church festivals
of one kind and another.   We saw Pius IX
(to whom the liberals everywhere were still
looking as friendly to their cause) on two

occasions, a man with so benignant a face that no one who saw him could expect from him anything but benevolence and love. We first saw him in the Sistine Chapel on Ash Wednesday, when with the impressive ceremonial of his church he placed the ashes on the heads of the cardinals and on that of the Duke of Norfolk, the great English Catholic. I remember distinctly the marked face of Cardinal Antonelli who became the dominant adviser of the Pope. He had brilliant eyes, a swarthy complexion, and an expression that put you on your guard against his strategy. One act in the service produced a comical effect on us who had never witnessed the ceremonial before. When the Cardinals kneeled as a prayer was offered, a page stepped behind each and twisted the tail of his gown into a knot, exactly as we tie a horse's tail into a knot in muddy weather.

One morning with a large assembly we stood in St. Peter's, waiting for the Pope to appear before the high altar for a great ceremonial. Distinguished representatives from all civilized lands were present. At last the doors from the Vatican approach swung open, the song from the choir broke upon the ear, and the Holy Father appeared borne in a sort of palanquin. As the attention of the multitude was absorbed by the scene, a man standing by my side pointed to a beautiful Italian boy near us and said, "It is hard, is it not, to realize that this little body is a temple greater than that in which we stand?"

A drive to Tivoli and the sight of the "Praeceps Anio" gave us one of our most delightful days.

The visit to Rome brought to me the first real revelation of the arts of sculpture and painting. The galleries and churches opened to me a new world. One can not describe what it was to a person who had no conception of art except what he had derived from the sight of Powers' Greek Slave and copies in private houses of two or three classical masterpieces of painting, to have suddenly spread before him the immeasurable artistic wealth of Rome, with full liberty to gaze upon it at will and to attain to some worthy appreciation of its wealth. Life could never again be quite what it was before. Of all the gifts of Rome to me that was the greatest.

During our stay in Rome the diligence on the journey between Rome and Florence was several times stopped by highwaymen, and the passengers were robbed of their money, watches, and jewels. It was said that the robbers were for the most part men of good families. Certainly they showed good breeding. They usually begged the passengers to fear no bodily harm. They said that they regretted extremely that the stress of the revolutionary period had forced them to resort to this means of gaining a livelihood. They politely helped the ladies to alight, and after receiving their jewels and money politely handed them back to the carriage.

We four, who found the travelling from Naples with the *vetturino* so pleasant, employed him to take us to Florence. We were six days on the journey, going by Perugia, and a most agreeable journey it was. We encountered no highwaymen.

Of course the galleries at Florence chiefly absorbed our attention. But the political situation was extremely interesting. The Austrians were in possession of Tuscany. They were intensely hated by the Italians. We had rooms on the great Piazza del Gran Duca.

Twice a week Austrian troops assembled there and their attractive bands discoursed most charming music. But as the troops passed along the streets the shutters were closed and on the Piazza not a Florentine could be seen. The foreigners and the Austrians had the music to themselves. On the occasion of a church festival we saw the Grand Duke and members of his family in garb of penitence, marching at the head of the procession. But on his approach the streets were deserted.

We went via Bologna and Padua to Venice where we spent some days in that delight which Venice brings to every traveller. The city seems to me to have changed less since that time than any other Italian city of importance.

We sailed thence to Trieste and then made the long journey by diligence, travelling day and night, to Gratz, which was even then a flourishing, manufacturing city, though we like most Americans had hardly known of its existence. From Gratz we were able to go by rail to Vienna. Partly because we had friends there, we spent several days in the Austrian capital.

We were fortunate enough to be there on what was called the Day of the Three Emperors. There was a military celebration of the suppression of the rebellion of Hungary. The three sovereigns present were the Austrian Emperor, Francis Joseph, the Russian Emperor, Nicholas, and the Prussian King, William. Fifteen thousand troops were assembled on the Glacis. The Emperor Nicholas took command and ordered the manœuvres. He looked the Emperor more than any man I ever saw. Of the gigantic Romanoff stature, of commanding mien, he sat upon his powerful horse as though ready in a joust to meet any foe.[1] As after the manœuvres were ended the troops marched through the principal streets, they were preceded not only by the sovereigns and a large number of generals but also by the ladies of the Imperial Austrian family in their open carriages. Though we young Americans, never having seen so many men under arms, were impressed by the brilliant display, yet our sympathy with the Hungarians whom the Austrian government had been enabled only by Russian help to defeat, led us to look on with an inward protest, especially as we had seen the breaches in the city walls which the Hungarian revolutionists had made with their cannon as they were on the point of gaining their independence.

In these later years, when the affectionate loyalty of the Austrians to Francis

---

[1] On the day before this parade we visited the Imperial stables. Noticing one horse standing in his stable with two heavy sacks on his back, we were told that he was to bear the Emperor Nicholas, and was in training for the unaccustomed load, as the Emperor weighed two hundred and forty pounds.

Joseph has apparently saved the Empire from dissolution, I have often recalled the statements made to me by a highly intelligent Viennese during this visit. He said that the young Emperor who had recently come to the throne was really hated then by the populace for his cruel and overbearing manner. He gave as an illustration the statement that a student crossing the Glacis in a snow storm with his head down did not see the Emperor who was passing, and so did not salute him, and that the Emperor was so affronted that he caused the innocent offender to be flogged. Whether this report was true, I cannot say. But that it could be circulated indicated a feeling utterly different from that which his subjects now cherish towards him.

While at Vienna I received a letter from President Wayland, offering me as I might prefer either the Chair of Civil Engineering or that of the Modern Languages in Brown University, with permission to remain abroad a year and a half for the purpose of study. After deliberation, I decided to accept the Chair of Modern Languages. My throat had so far regained its strength that I thought I could venture to try the experiment of teaching.

We made brief visits at Prague, Dresden, Berlin, and Cologne on our way to Paris. Here Mr. Hazard left me on June 10, 1852, and returned home via England. I began the search for a teacher of French. After a little I had the good fortune to make the acquaintance of Monsieur Jansen who had once been a Professor in a Lycée, but had been thrown out of office owing to his radical republicanisn, He was a guileless, scholarly man, without much skill in making his way in the world, especially in the troublous times which had come to France. He detested Louis Napoleon and all his followers and believed that the eyes of spies were always upon him. He had a charming wife, one of the best type of the intelligent, well-bred, frugal woman of the middle class, and a diffident gentle daughter of eighteen years. Into this charming household I was permitted to come as a boarder and a pupil. It was a surprising revelation to me who, like most young Americans, had formed my ideas of French domestic life from sensational stories of Parisian adventures, to see the beautiful simplicity of this quiet and virtuous French home. I soon learned that this was not an exceptional home. Perhaps in no particular have English and Americans been so far astray in their judgments of the French people as in respect to the purity of their domestic life.

Monsieur Jansen lived in Passy, on the Avenue de St. Cloud, just outside of the Arc de Triomphe de l'Etoile. It was an easy stroll to the Bois de Boulogne, whither I often went with my books. Frequently with the family I went on a picnic to St. Cloud or some other attractive spot. On Sundays I usually went to the Church of the Oratoire, where I heard some of the most eloquent Protestant preachers. One peculiar, but rather commendable custom of the preachers, which I have never seen spoken of in books, I noticed with interest. Their style was picturesque or dramatic. After an eloquent passage which closed one division or head of the sermon, the preacher would pause to clear his throat or use his handkerchief, and the whole congregation availed themselves of that opportunity to do the same thing. Then as he proceeded, he was not interrupted by coughing. In due time he paused again for the same purpose, and the congregation imitated him once more. Occasionally I went to the Sorbonne or the Collège de France and heard lectures. But in the main I gave my attention to writing French and conversing and reading French literature. One interesting and instructive diversion was after reading French history to go to Versailles and see the historical pictures which adorn the walls.

In October, 1852, I left Paris for Germany. I travelled through Holland and went to Braunschweig to study German. I found an excellent home in the house of Herr Sack, the clerk of the Circuit Court, an elderly man who had fought in the Battle of Waterloo and was a somewhat noted local antiquary. His eldest daughter, who was a teacher in a private school and was a scholar of large reading in English as well as in German literature, became my teacher. She was most competent. I have always regarded myself as so greatly indebted to her that I continued correspondence with her until her death in 1907. I know few American women who can recite so many fine passages from English poets as she could. I was impressed by this and other facts with the excellent literary training which the German schools gave their girls,

One book from the father's pen was a striking illustration of the German thoroughness (Gründlichkeit), which I had occasion so often to remark in German writers. In early times the Brunswickers of wealth and rank placed elaborate family

coats-of-arms on their chimneys in conspicuous positions. Herr Sack found in
these with their mottoes a valuable contribution to the history of the city. So he
wrote a book on the History of the Chimneys of Brunswick. It was divided into
two parts. In order to lay a proper foundation for his interpretation of the sym-
bols, he devoted the first part to the history
of chimneys in Greece and Rome and there
reached the conclusion that the Greeks and
Romans had no chimneys. Not till he had
done this was he prepared to discuss the
History of Chimneys in Brunswick.

So far as I could learn I was the first
American ever known in Brunswick. One
South American from Bogotá arrived there
before me. But as people generally knew
nothing of Bogotá, he used in company to
draw near to me, throw his arm across my
shoulder, and say somewhat ostentatiously,
"Ach! wir sind Amerikaner."

I was invited to join a club of German
gentlemen who met occasionally to speak
English and who wished me to correct their
expressions when necessary. It so happened that for some time the only member
to whom English was vernacular was a
mechanical engineer from London, connected with the railway. He was illiterate

and his speech was pure cockney. I was soon embarrassed by their remarking the differences between his speech and mine, and asking for explanations. These I gave when he was not present.

"Uncle Tom's Cabin" by Mrs. Stowe appeared while I was in Brunswick, and was read with great eagerness. But many of my acquaintances were puzzled by Topsy's English, and could find no help in their dictionaries. For a time I could scarcely take a walk on the street without being accosted, occasionally by strangers to whom I had been pointed out as an American, for aid in interpreting the negro dialect.

In this connection I am tempted to describe an adventure which befell me in a school to which English and Irish girls of good families had been sent to learn German. The proprietor of the school was a relative of the Sacks with whom I was living. So I was invited with them to a Christmas supper at the school. I was seated at the table at a safe distance from the girls who appeared to be from fourteen to eighteen years of age. At the close of the supper I was surprised to receive, through the host, a request from the girls that I would say a few words in American. It had not occurred to me that they could be ignorant of the fact that English is our vernacular. But as it appeared that they were, I thought an innocent trick was allowable. So I arose and made a speech in what in my childhood we boys called "hog Latin." It consists in beginning a word with the last syllable and then recurring to the first: *e.g.*, the word "German" would appear as "man-o-ger." Of course there was resemblance enough in some words to the real words so that they would catch a little of what I was saying. But they were much bewildered. And the German hearers were even more so. I sat down amid hearty applause. The young ladies sent up an expression of thanks. I never explained the trick to my German friends until I went to Brunswick forty years later.

The tenor singer in the Brunswick Opera Company and his wife occupied a room directly under mine. He was a very genial, jolly fellow, and I used often to walk with him. Through him I made the acquaintance in his rooms of his associates in the Opera Company. As the members of the company hold permanent positions in a German city, I met them at times in general society. They presented to me a new side of life. I found them very companionable and entertaining, but was surprised to observe that most of them had very limited attainments beyond their professional training. The breath of their life seemed to be public applause of their performances, and perhaps as a consequence of this they were very jealous of each other's success. Most of them mingled with their neighbours without attracting more especial attention than other respectable citizens.

I spent a pleasant afternoon with Herr Sack, visiting the great library at Wolfenbüttel, then in charge of an aged librarian who, though utterly blind, could lay his hand on any book he sought in the great collection.

It was on the whole a most profitable and enjoyable winter that I spent in Brunswick. In April, 1853, I left the circle of friends, by whom I had been most hospitably received, with sincere regret, in order to attend lectures on modern German literature at the University of Berlin.

I took lodgings near the middle of the city. I was disappointed in applying at the University to find that there was no course to be given on the subject I wished to study. I sent to several Universities and could learn of no such course except at Munich. While I was busy in this quest, and was seeking to procure from the city authorities the ordinary permission to occupy lodgings, I was surprised to be informed by the police officers who had received my passport that I could not receive that permission in the usual form. On the contrary I was directed to report twice a week in person at the police office. In answer to my inquiry for the reason of this extraordinary demand, I was told that revolutionists with the spirit of 1848 were busy, that bombs and other munitions had been found in the attic of a storehouse, and that Germans bearing American passports were supposed to be coming to town to engage in lawless enterprises. "Well," I said, "how does that concern me?" "Well, we thought you might be one of these Germans." "It is very flattering," I replied, "to be regarded by you as a German. Will you not be good enough to tell me why you have taken me for a German?" "Well," was the reply, "you have a square head and light hair and complexion, in short, look like a German." "But," I rejoined, "you must see that I do not speak your language like a German. I have been in your country only a few months." "Yes," said the official, "but the foreign accent could be assumed."

I could not argue against "Caesar with his ten legions." After a week's sojourn under these conditions, reflecting that only in Munich could I find the lectures I wanted, I resolved to go there. So I went to the police office and demanded my passport, viséd for Munich. To my surprise and to my temporary satisfaction the officer could not find it. I saw at once that there I had him at my mercy. In those days a passport was regarded in official circles as such a sacrosanct document that a police official could hardly commit a more serious offence than to lose it. So I assumed the menacing air, and told him that if the passport was not at my room viséd within three hours I would report the case to the American Chargé for complaint to the Government. It was delivered to me within the time and I set out for Munich.

On the way I spent a day or two with intense delight at Nuremburg, in which it was so easy to reproduce in imagination the mediaeval life of Hans Sachs' time. I also stopped at Augsburg.

At Munich the police office at first declined to give me permission to reside, because in my application I wrote out my middle name in full, while my passport contained merely the initial letter of my middle name. It required an argument to convince the stupid official of my identity.

One of my first pleasures in Munich was that of hearing the great chemist Liebig lecture. Of all the professors I heard, he was the most attractive in manner. It proved to be his son-in-law, Moritz Carrière, who gave the course in modern German literature which I came to hear. I wanted especially to listen to discourses on Lessing, Goethe, and Schiller. As I had six weeks at my disposal, and Carrière was announced for three lectures a week, I hoped I might get some valuable instruction. He was an excellent lecturer. But alas! the old German "Gründlichkeit," if not so striking as that of Herr Sack in his "History of the Chimneys of Brunswick," proved fatal. For he began back with the Germans of whom I had read in the Germania of Tacitus, and in my six weeks had only got down towards the modern times as far as the translation of the Bible by Ulfilas. However, I heard other excellent lectures on the Ancient Classics, and enjoyed much the visits to the galleries of art. My sojourn was not without profit and pleasure.

From Munich I went to Zürich. After a short stay there I crossed the lake and walked over the Brünig Pass to Thun and

Berne, and travelled thence by diligence to Geneva and thence by diligence and rail to Paris. I received a hearty welcome from my old friends, the Jansens, with whom I remained about six weeks. During this sojourn in Paris I had the pleasure of meeting at dinner at the house of a friend, Monsieur Sainte-Beuve, the great critic, whose writings had greatly attracted me. He was most genial and interesting. He was of medium height, inclined to *embonpoint*, and for some reason which I should be puzzled to explain reminded me of the picture I had always formed to myself of the poet Horace.

From Paris in July I made a hurried journey through England, spending a week in London, then passing by Stratford, Warwick, Oxford, and York, to Edinburgh and Glasgow and to Liverpool, whence I sailed on July 29 for Philadelphia. We had a wonderfully smooth voyage. The steamer soon sailed on her return voyage, and was never heard from. I stopped in New York, where the first of our national expositions was being held. I remember seeing a good farmer and his wife gazing on the casts of Thorwaldsen's Christ and the Apostles, and concluding after some discussion that they were the Presidents of the United States.

I reached my father's house in Scituate after an absence of nearly two years. I learned that both my maternal grandparents had died since my last letters had reached me abroad. I was especially grieved at the death of my grandmother. It was from her that my dear mother inherited most of her traits.

IV

THE PROFESSORSHIP IN BROWN UNIVERSITY AND EDITORSHIP OF THE PROVIDENCE *JOURNAL*

I WAS twenty-four years of age when I entered on the duties of my professorship. I was the youngest member of the Faculty. Most of the professors had been my teachers. Professor Robinson P. Dunn, who had recently been called to the Chair of Rhetoric and English Literature, was only a few years my senior. He became at once my intimate companion and a most congenial associate in my studies. I was well aware that my preparation for my special work was less adequate than I could have desired. I purposed to return to Europe for further study as soon as I had liquidated the debt I had incurred in my sojourn in Europe. I was particularly desirous of studying the Italian language and literature. I had become deeply interested in tracing the influence of the leading European literatures on each other. I soon wrote articles for the *North American Review*,

under the encouragement of its scholarly
editor, Dr. Andrew P. Peabody, pointing
out to some extent the interaction of the
French, German, and English literatures.
I cherished the hope that on a visit to
Europe I might write a book of some
worth on the reciprocal influence of the
chief literatures on each other. Like many
another dream of early years that has remained only a dream. But, in my teaching, which was necessarily elementary, since
most of my students began the study of the
modern languages with me, I strove and
not without fair success, I hope, to imbue
them with some enthusiasm for the study
of the great authors to whom I introduced
them.

It was an interesting period in the history of the University when I entered upon
my official connection with it. President
Wayland, who was a pioneer in the reform
of our traditional collegiate system, had
induced the Corporation to make important
innovations. As early as 1842 he had published a small book entitled "Thoughts on
the Present Collegiate System in the United
States," in which he had pointed out what
he regarded as some of the defects in that
system. He maintained that the colleges
were not furnishing the education which

was needed to meet our wants, especially that they were not training men in science and its applications to life. The book attracted some attention, but not so much as it deserved.

Further observation and reflection confirmed him in the opinion that a change in the organization of our colleges ought to be attempted. In a report to the Trustees of Brown University in 1850 he so impressed them with his views that they raised a fund, large for those days, for the reorganization of the work of their institution in accordance with his ideas. He provided for more generous work in the sciences and in modern languages and in engineering and large liberty in the election of studies. He really opened the way for that broadening and liberalizing of collegiate study which in a few years prevailed to a considerable extent in every American college of standing. He was the pioneer who broke away from the old traditional path, which our colleges had followed from the seventeenth century, and pointed them to the road which they are now all following. The credit which is his due for this service he has not always received. The immediate consequence of the adoption of what was called the "new system" had been a large increase in the attendance, and a certain enthusiasm among the students about this new departure. This was favourable to the work in my department. Extension lectures, which have since been introduced by some universities in this country and in England in order to bring university instruction to the masses, were given by Professor Chase to the jewellers and by Professor Caswell to the mechanics in Providence. The college which had not been in close touch with the people of the State was brought nearer to them by lyceum lectures given by members of the Faculty. I went out frequently to lecture on "Life in Europe" and on education. But in spite of the enthusiasm with which Dr. Wayland and some of his friends gave a new impulse to the college, serious difficulties were encountered in carrying into effect his cherished plans. Some of the Professors had not much sympathy with his ideas of reform. The funds raised to carry the "new system" into operation, though regarded as adequate when they were raised, proved insufficient. The President finally became discouraged and resigned his place in 1855. He was succeeded by Dr. Sears, who was friendly to the traditional ideas of college work rather than to Dr. Wayland's. There-

fore from the time of his accession to office
the spirit of collegiate reform visibly lan-
guished. But the impulse which had been
given to the college was not wholly lost.
In the classes which I had the pleasure of
teaching, were not a few whose subsequent
careers reflected much honour on themsleves
and on the University. Most conspicuous
among them are Richard Olney of the class
of 1856, and John Hay, of the class of 1858.
Both gave marked promise. Mr. Olney,
afterwards Attorney-general and then Secretary of State of the United States, showed
the traits of mind which characterize the
profound lawyer. For Mr. Hay one would
have predicted a brilliant literary future.
I have often said that he was the most
felicitous translator I ever met in my
classes. He wrote verses of unusual merit
for an undergraduate. He was modest even
to diffidence, often blushing to the roots of
his hair when he rose to recite. In the
years of his middle life, and especially after
the production of his books on Spanish life,
written in so picturesque a style, I used in
common with many of his friends to regret
that circumstances had diverted him from
a purely literary career. But we all rejoice
now that Providence placed him in the chair
of Secretary of State, at a time when he could

be of such transcendent service to us and to the Eastern world. As I happened to be on the steamer with him when he was returning from the Embassy at London, I know from my conversation with him on the voyage that he entered on the duties of that high office with hesitancy and misgiving. He said to me, "I accepted it because it is an office that one can hardly refuse."

When I entered on the duties of the professorship, the curricula were so arranged that my students could carry the work in the modern languages and literatures to a somewhat advanced stage, and to my great satisfaction. But later changes were made which restricted my classes to one year's work in each of the languages. This elementary teaching soon became rather uninspiring to me. I used to say it did not seem to stretch the flexor muscles of the mind.

Partly owing to this fact, by an arrangement with Governor Anthony, editor and chief proprietor of the Providence *Journal*, while I was holding the chair in college, I wrote regularly leading articles, chiefly on foreign affairs. When he was elected to the United States Senate in 1858, I assumed responsibility, for 1859, of all the leading articles, while James S. Ham acted as managing editor. This attempt to carry both my college work and my editorial work did not prove satisfactory to me. During the year, Senator Anthony proposed that I should resign my position at the college and take the editorial charge of the newspaper. The college salary was very small and there seemed to be no prospect of an increase. The *Journal* held a very commanding position. The great questions which the North and South were soon to submit to the dread arbitrament of war were already under discussion. The field for earnest and patriotic editorial work was very inviting. I decided to exchange the professor's chair for the editor's.

I was called on at various times to give lectures in and near Providence. I first wrote out some lectures and read them. I soon found that this was not the most effective mode of lecturing and moreover that it made too great a draught on my throat. So I decided to throw away manuscript. I thus acquired the habit of speaking without notes, which I have followed through my life with few exceptions and then against my wishes. Many of my speeches I have after delivery reduced to writing in order to preserve them; but the pleasure and effectiveness of speaking without reading can never be equalled by reading a manuscript.

It was during the period of my official connection with Brown University on November 26, 1855, that I was married to Sarah Swoope Caswell, only daughter of Rev. Alexis Caswell, D.D., for many years Professor in the University and afterwards its President. This was the most fortunate event in my life. She was eminently fitted to be my helpmeet in all the various experiences of our lives. If I have achieved any degree of success, I owe it largely to her.

The spirit in which Mr. Anthony had always conducted the *Journal* was that of courtesy towards opponents and of optimism concerning the country. Three things he insisted on: first, the *Journal* should be a clean paper, even in its advertisements; second, the English should be pure; third, whatever the *Journal* could do for the honour, the prosperity, the glory of Rhode Island should be done at any sacrifice. For us who were left in his absence to carry on the work it was the tradition and the law to let his spirit prevail, so far as we could attain to it, in all departments of the paper. Accordingly at the end of the academic year, 1859–60, I resigned my chair

[112]

in the college and accepted the invitation to take the editorship, subject of course to the control of the Senator. That position I held from the summer of 1860 to the summer of 1866. A more interesting and important period for the responsible post of conducting such a newspaper has not been presented in our history. Few of the newspapers in the country have so won the confidence and so controlled the opinions of their constituency as the Providence *Journal* under the editorship of Henry B. Anthony. Its opponents used to say that its readers considered it their political bible, and opened it in the morning to know what they ought to think. The opportunity, the privilege, the duty of such a journal at such an epoch, no one comprehended more thoroughly than Senator Anthony. Never was there a more indulgent chief. He left us in the offices the utmost liberty compatible with the general policy of the paper. Though with my limited experience I must have made mistakes, I do not remember that he ever complained to me or ever criticized me, except as criticisms may sometimes have been gently implied in suggestions.

Those who now enter the spacious offices of the *Journal* and see its large mechanical outfit and its force of writers, reporters, and clerks, will have difficulty in understanding on how modest a scale it was then conducted. The efficient clerk at the desk in the counting room was the only accountant. I not only wrote as a rule all the editorial articles, but read all the exchanges and made the clippings and supervised and edited all communications. We had no regular reporter except the marine reporter who was a compositor and set up all the news he gathered. When I wished a reporter I sent out and found one. Two or three college students held themselves subject to my call when I could find them. After the war came on I engaged some young officer in each Rhode Island regiment and battery, generally one of my college pupils, to send correspondence from the front. Not infrequently, after I had gone home at a late hour, the foreman of the printing office receiving some important war news, brought it to my house and I crept out of bed and in very slender attire wrote an article for him to take back.

In respect to the questions which engaged public attention in the months preceding the war, I, like most young men, shared the views of the more radical wing of the Republican party in Rhode Island. But the business relations of our cotton brokers and manufacturers in that State with the South had been so close that a large portion, perhaps a majority, of the party were very conservative, and ready to concede much to the South to avoid a conflict. Some of the elderly citizens of wealth and influence from time to time laboured earnestly with me to convince me of my errors and to persuade me to commit the paper to a less dangerous policy.

The election of a governor of the State was the occasion of a rupture in the party. A worthy grocer, Mr. Seth Padelford, by active canvassing secured the gubernatorial nomination at the Republican State Convention, and in accordance with usage the *Journal* supported him as the regular nominee. His nomination was distasteful to a large number of the prominent Republicans in Providence. They persuaded William Sprague, a wealthy young manufacturer, to accept a nomination against him. One of the principal arguments which they adduced for opposing Padelford was that he had at some time given a hundred dollars to circulate a volume written by Hinton Rowan Helper of North Carolina, to show that on economic grounds slavery was injurious to the South. This was loudly proclaimed as a proof that Mr. Padelford was an abolitionist and so unfriendly to the South. I believe Mr. Padelford had in fact never read the book. Of course it fell to me to make as good a fight for him against many of the old friends of the *Journal* as I could. The strong bank account of the Spragues was heavily drawn upon, and Mr. Padelford who spent his money freely was defeated.

During the campaign two or three gentlemen, who were managing the Sprague campaign, waited on me and asked if the *Journal* could be bought. (They had no newspaper then.) I replied that I did not own it, but that I presumed that like other property it could be bought if enough was offered for it. They talked on for some time rather vaguely, until at last it appeared that they did not care to buy it unless I was bought with it. When I discovered this I replied, holding up my quill pen, "As I have said, I presume you can buy the *Journal*, but the Spragues have not money enough to buy this quill." Whereupon they withdrew.

Another interesting incident occurred in the campaign. We invited Abraham Lincoln to make a speech in Providence. He had come to New York to give his Address, now so famous, which shows that the Fathers of the Republic lived in the hope of the ultimate extinction of slavery. He was an entire stranger in Providence; and when he appeared on the stage with his long, lank figure, his loose frock coat, his hair just cut rather close, his homely face, we were rather disappointed. But as he proceeded with his speech our solicitude disappeared. It so happened that I sat by the side of the editor of the Democratic paper, Welcome B. Sayles.[1] At the close of the address he said to me, "That is the finest constitutional argument for a popular audience that I ever heard." And certainly I agreed with him.

It was not long before the speaker was nominated for the Presidency. Rhode Island like other Eastern states had hoped for the nomination of Seward. And when the news of Lincoln's nomination came, we recalled that awkward figure which we had seen in Railroad Hall, and heard the commendations of him as a rail-splitter, and we wondered whether he was to prove the leader we needed for the trying days we were expecting. So keen was the disappointment in the State that

[1] Mr. Sayles afterwards went to the war as Colonel of the Seventh Rhode Island regiment, and was killed.

clearly an effort was needed to secure him earnest support.

I bethought myself of one source of help. I remembered that John Hay, my old pupil, was a student of law in Lincoln's office. I wrote to him, explaining the situation and asking him to write a few letters about Lincoln, which would help me in awakening enthusiasm. He complied with my request, but he was so accustomed to look at Lincoln with western eyes that he dwelt unduly for my purpose on the qualities which had made him so popular in Illinois. I "edited" his writing severely and published it. What would I not give now for the original manuscript which went to the waste basket with other copy!

During the war the labour of editing was very severe but intensely interesting. The breach in the Republican party was healed, and finally Mr. Padelford was elected Governor, largely by the aid of the supporters of Sprague. I found the annoyance of editorial life much less than I had anticipated. The office was the gathering place for all the prominent men in the state. My practice was to write in the outer room surrounded by these men. I was thus able to feel the public pulse every day and to get many excellent suggestions from the conversation.

I used jocosely to say to some of these bright men that "I milked every cow that came into my enclosure."

I recall with interest visits to the office of many prominent men, among them Charles Sumner, Schuyler Colfax, Henry J. Raymond, Editor of the New York *Times*, Horace Greeley, and Governor Andrew. Of all these the most stimulating to the young editor was Governor Andrew, with his lofty enthusiasms and great good sense. Mr. Greeley having once asked for a place where he could write, I offered him my table, which was of the usual height. "You don't write at such a table as that, do you?" said he. "Let me have some books to pile on it." I piled up on it the bound volumes of the Congressional Record, until when he was seated they reached to his chin, and on top he spread his paper and wrote.

After George W. Danielson in 1863 became connected with the *Journal*, the supervision of the business, of the printing, of the local reporting, and of the evening edition, called the *Bulletin*, was assumed by him. Perhaps I may properly say now that he and I conceived the idea of purchasing, if practicable, the *Journal* and publishing it as a non-partisan independent newspaper. But Senator Anthony was unwilling to sell.

In 1866 the severity of the work in which I had really been engaged for eight years, with only a week's vacation in each year, was beginning to affect my health. An urgent call to return to academic life led me to accept the presidency of the University of Vermont in August of that year. But my experience of newspaper life has been of great service to me in all my subsequent career. Editorial work trains one to both readiness and accuracy in writing. One learns to say on the first trial exactly what one means to say, and to avoid diffuseness. One who has a responsible charge in the conduct of a newspaper has large opportunities to understand men and to test his own courage in standing for what is right and conducive to the public good, especially when in his opinions he differs from some of his friends. It was not without much reluctance that I decided to abandon editorial life and return to academic work.

V

THE PRESIDENCY OF THE UNIVER-
SITY OF VERMONT

THE University of Vermont, founded in
1791, though a small college, had an honourable history. Its standard of work
compared favourably always with the better
New England colleges. Eminent scholars
had held places in its Faculty. President
James Marsh, one of the first Americans to
commend Coleridge to us, was one of the
most gifted philosophers this country has
produced. President Wheeler, Professor
Joseph Torrey, the translator of Neander,
Professor Shedd, afterward a member of the
Faculty of the Union Theological Seminary in New York, and Professor George
W. Benedict, a most energetic adminis-
trator, had given to the college a reputation
which attracted students from beyond the
boundaries of the State. It had a good
proportion of eminent graduates.

The Civil War, however, had broken its
strength. A large number of its students
entered the army, and the boys in the
academies were diverted from college to the

[121]

public service. The resources of the institution declined. Its friends became despondent. Some thought it must die.

But when the so-called Morrill Bill, establishing Agricultural Colleges, was passed, the trustees decided to accept the endowment offered to Vermont and to organize the college in connection with the University. Senator Morrill became one of the trustees. Some of the old classical graduates feared the result.

My task was to organize the Agricultural College and effect a harmonious union with the old college, to aid in raising funds which it was clearly seen were needed, and to inspire the public and especially the alumni with the confident belief that the Institution really had a future.

This required all the energy and enthusiasm which I could command. In some measure the college had drifted away from the people in Burlington, owing to their despondency about it. One of the first steps my wife and I took was to bring the citizens into close social relations with the college. The addition of cultivated young men to the Faculty made this easy. I then improved every opportunity to visit schools, to lecture in many towns, to address the county and state fairs on agricultural education, in fact to beat the bushes from one end of the state to the other in order to convince the public that we were alive and were especially desirous to do something for the farmers. I need hardly add they were the hardest class to convince that we could be of any help to them. With an associate from the Trustees or from the Faculty, I visited Boston, New York, and Washington, to obtain subscriptions. I remember with pleasure as soon as we reached Washington, Henry J. Raymond, who was an alumnus, gathered five other alumni in Congress in front of the Speaker's desk, before the session opened, and after making a handsome subscription himself, induced them all to subscribe. Thaddeus Stevens was one of them.

As we had not funds enough to complete our Faculty, I set myself to teach the branches not provided for, namely, Rhetoric, History, German, and International Law.

The persons who were of the most assistance to me in this work of raising money and awakening the state were Grenville G. Benedict, Secretary of the Corporation, and Professor Buckham, who filled the place of President after I left, until his death in 1910.

In all that strenuous life there were some amusing experiences. I was speaking one day at the State Fair at Brattleboro. As I sat down, a gentleman planted himself squarely before me and exclaimed, "Sir, how old are you?" I was a little surprised at being accosted thus by a stranger. Suddenly it occurred to me that the State Lunatic Asylum was in that town, and I said to myself, "This is some harmless patient to whom they have allowed liberty." So I said to him, "Sir, how old are you?" He replied, "I am thirty-eight." I then said, "That is exactly my age." He went away satisfied. I learned on inquiry that he was pastor of a church in the town.

Afterwards in Vermont, I was repeatedly asked when introduced to a stranger, how old I was. I know of no explanation, out of China, for such a usage, except that some of the recent Presidents had been advanced in years and infirm, and there was genuine surprise at seeing one so young as I was.

I also once learned how much it was worth to attend the funeral of a relative who was a benefactor of the college. A man who had given his little property to endow some scholarships on condition the college should pay his board with a nephew and niece so long as he lived, finally died. I attended the funeral. The nephew and niece accompanied the body some miles with me to the burial. I told them to send me the bill for the funeral expenses. When it came it contained a *per diem* charge for the time consumed in going to the burial. I ordered the treasurer to pay that bill, since it was worth the price to learn what one can earn in attending a relative's funeral.

When I went to Burlington, I found in force a rule that any student who in his whole college course should have ten unexcused absences must be expelled. I said at once, "That is a foolish rule. What will happen is that you will excuse the tenth absence. However, until we change the rule, I will enforce it."

A rather slack, self-indulgent boy came to me to be excused to attend his grandmother's funeral. He had nine unexcused absences. But of course I excused him. In two weeks he came to be excused to attend another grandmother's funeral. As he might have two grandmothers, I excused him again. Judge of my surprise when in two weeks more he came to be excused to attend another grandmother's funeral. "How is this," I said, "You have been to two grandmother's funerals." "Yes." he replied, "This is my step-father's mother." "I see," said I, "but mark my word, if you have another grandmother's funeral, you will leave college." He graduated.

The administration of a college with a small number of students taught me certain lessons. It gave me peculiar pleasure from my intimate personal acquaintance with each pupil and in many cases with his parents. Since I also taught every one in more than one branch, I was able to guide and impress them all, to direct their reading and writing and help shape their character and their plans as would have been quite impossible in a large institution. The relations thus established between me and them have been a source of permanent gratification to me and I trust to not a few of them.

Nor can I refrain from recalling the friendship formed with two eminent citizens of Burlington, which proved of lasting pleasure and service to me. I refer to Senator Edmunds and the Honourable E. J. Phelps, afterwards Minister to Great Britain. They were the leading lawyers of Vermont. Senator Edmunds showed in his long public service the powers of a great statesman, and to the great regret of the nation withdrew too early from official life. Mr. Phelps was one of the most brilliant minds whom it has been my fortune to know. Unhappily during most of his life he was on the wrong side in politics to be called into public service. They both lent a charm to social life in Burlington, which makes me look back on it as a good fortune to have dwelt there with them.

Though I lived in Vermont only five years, I formed a wide acquaintance in the State, and became strongly attached to the people. They were an agricultural community of the best type. Serious, earnest, industrious, frugal, they formed their opinions with deliberation, and adhered to them firmly. Their moral and religious ideals were high. The sons of Vermont, scattered far and wide through the land, reflect great honour upon her.

The university has received generous gifts from its alumni and other friends and has enjoyed great prosperity under President Buckham.[1]

[1] He died November 29, 1910, after thirty-nine years of service as President. He has been succeeded by Dr. Guy Potter Benton.

VI

THE MISSION TO CHINA[1]

On February 20, 1880, I received a letter from Hon. H. P. Baldwin, a Senator from Michigan, informing me that Mr. Evarts, Secretary of State, desired to see me at an early date in Washington on a matter of public interest. It occurred to me as possible that he wished me to take a place on a commission to consider either the Fisheries Question or the Isthmian Interoceanic Canal Question.

I soon went to Washington, and with Senator Baldwin called on the Secretary by appointment at his house. I learned from him that my friend Senator Edmunds of Vermont had some months before directed his attention to me as a suitable person for diplomatic service.

The Secretary soon made it known to me that he desired me to go to China as one of

[1] Though I went from Vermont to the University of Michigan in 1870, it seems most convenient to defer the narrative of my life in Michigan until after the description of my experience in public life, and of two journeys to Europe.

two Commissioners (the other to be a Californian), to secure, if possible, a revision of our treaties with that Empire, especially with the purpose of restraining in some degree the emigration which was threatening to flood the Pacific States. He dwelt on the importance of adjusting this Asiatic life to ours in some way best both for the Chinese and for us. His manner and conversation were most charming. A vein of humour ran through his gravest talk like a vein of silver through the rock. To my inquiry whether he had any reason to suppose the Chinese were ready to accede to his propositions, he replied that General Grant had, in his interviews with high Chinese officials, received the impression that they were ready to take some steps in that direction. He added then in his inimitable way, "I should not be surprised if the Chinese should be entirely willing. They may well say, ' You are asking us to abide by our own doctrines. We always told you that we did not wish to open so intimate intercourse with you western nations. But you forced us at the cannon's mouth. You see we were right.'" Continuing, he said, "Perhaps we had better not despise a government which for thirty centuries has ruled a nation now numbering

[129]

three hundred millions, while we have only fifty millions, and they 'run us.'"

At the proper time I took occasion to say that I thought the Consular history of Rome was rather full of warnings against the policy of employing a commission of two, and that one of three would be more likely to accomplish a result, at any rate, to avoid an even decision. Later, Senator Edmunds advanced the same opinion, and finally a Commission of three was decided on.

At the close of the interview, the Secretary took me to the White House to see President Hayes. He seemed deeply impressed with the importance of restraining the immigration of the Chinese. I asked if the government supposed the country east of the Rocky Mountains was ready to adopt measures restrictive of Chinese immigration. In reply I was given to understand that the action of such a Commission as they were trying to appoint would of itself have much weight in securing acquiescence in reasonable measures.

After conference with Senators Edmunds, Anthony, Baldwin, and Ferry, I promised the Secretary that I would return home, give the subject full consideration, consult the Regents of the University, and give him answer at an early day.

On March 11, I wrote to the Secretary to the following effect: that if direct and formal prohibition of Chinese immigration was desired I preferred that some one else should undertake the work, but that if correction of the abuses now connected with the immigration was desired, and this correction should work as a restraint on the immigration, I was willing to undertake the task. He promptly replied that there was nothing in my letter incompatible with the purposes of the President, and he desired to send in my name to the Senate at once. April 9, I was confirmed as Minister and also as Chairman of the Commission for revising treaties with China. John F. Swift of California and William H. Trescot of South Carolina were appointed Commissioners.

On April 1, I had interesting interviews in Washington with Dr. Peter Parker, formerly medical missionary at Canton, and with George Bancroft, the historian. Both of them were opposed to unlimited immigration of the Chinese. Mr. Bancroft said he did not want to see the young men in Massachusetts towns forced to compete with the Chinese who had such low standards of living. He was also not without fear that the South might employ them and virtually reinstate a quasi-servitude.

On May 26, in response to a summons from Mr. Evarts, I reported in company with Mr. Trescot at his office in the expectation of receiving instructions. We had very charming interviews with him on four successive days. He discoursed at length on the various problems, which our relations with China have forced upon us, the difference between European and Asiatic immigration, the commercial questions involved in the Lekin tax, the importance of having an American policy, not tied to England, the expediency of dispersing the Chinese in our country, the importance of impressing the Chinese government with our desire to be fair and even generous towards them, and the question whether we can modify the treaty stipulations concerning ex-territoriality. All this did not result in furnishing us any specific instructions as to what we should demand in a treaty. But the Secretary informed us that definite instructions would overtake us on our journey.

On June 4, prominent citizens of Detroit gave a dinner in my honour. The Hon. George V. N. Lothrop, the most prominent member of the Michigan Bar, afterwards our Minister to Russia, presided with his characteristic grace. I would gladly have been excused from this reception, but my friends persuaded me that it would be helpful to the University. In my remarks I carefully refrained from discussing the questions which I was about to act on officially.

On the next day at 4 P.M., the Faculties and the students gave me a hearty reception in University Hall.

On June 6, with my wife and daughter and youngest son, I started for San Francisco and arrived there on the 11th, and remained until the 19th. We received many hospitalities. Mr. Trescot had reached there before me and Mr. Swift resided there. Especially profitable were interviews with the Chinese Consul and with Mr. Low, who had long been our minister to China. Apparently there was a general feeling that the coming of Chinese labourers should be limited, but not absolutely forbidden. One representative of the Labour Unions asked prohibition of immigration in order to protect American mechanics. I asked him if he could name one mechanic who had been crowded out of employment by the Chinese, and he confessed he could not.

On June 19, we sailed on the " Oceanic." In the voyage of eighteen days we did not, after leaving the California coast, see a

single vessel until we approached the coast
of Japan. We entered the harbour of
Yokohama at five o'clock in the morning.
Before the steamer had stopped, Japanese
boats, filled with half-naked boatmen,
swarmed about us to take passengers ashore.
Hardly had we dropped anchor before
Lieutenant Wainwright (now Admiral)
came on board to learn when I would receive
a call from Admiral Patterson, who was in
command of the United States squadron in
the harbour. At half-past nine he and
Captain Johnson, commanding the gun-
boat, "Ashuelot" called. Under orders from
our government they were waiting to take
us to China on the "Richmond" and the
"Ashuelot." As on our arrival they were
not quite ready to depart, we had the pleasure of spending ten days in Yokohama and
Tokio.

In view of the discussion which has been
carried on for some years concerning the
expediency of erecting houses at the expense
of our government for the residences of our
ministers and ambassadors, it may not be
amiss to report a conversation I had with
Judge Bingham, our minister to Japan at the
time of my visit. Observing that he was
living in a comfortable though modest
house, I asked him if he had built it at his

own expense. He said, "Oh, no. As we have ex-territoriality here, I was obliged to ask for an appropriation for a jail. I asked my old friends in Congress for an appropriation so liberal that I was able to build my house as an annex to the jail." He then took me to the rear of the house and showed me a prisoner confined in the room which was the jail.

Judge Bingham prided himself on having broken away from blindly following England, as most of the other ministers had. He said he had seen Sir Harry Parkes, the British minister shake his fist under the nose of the minister of Foreign Affairs. He added that the forcible withdrawal of a German vessel from quarantine was really stimulated by the Englishman.

On July 19, my family and I embarked on the United States gunboat "Ashuelot," Captain Johnson, for Shanghai. We stopped at Kobe and visited the old capital, Kioto. The Italian ship of war, " Vettor Pisani," under command of the Duke of Genoa, was at Kobe. We exchanged calls with him and found him very cordial and simple in his manners. He preferred to be addressed simply as Captain. The sail through the Inland Sea was charming. It reminded one of Lake Champlain and Lake George.

We arrived at Shanghai on July 27, and were the guests of Consul-General Denny. I was told that Rev. Dr. Yates, an American missionary of the Southern Baptist Society, knew the Chinamen better than any other foreigner in the city. I therefore asked him for a description of the Chinaman. He said he had studied the Chinaman many years. At times he flattered himself that he had come to understand thoroughly the Chinaman's nature to the very bottom. But just as he began to inflate himself with complacency at his achievement, some new depth in the Chinaman's nature yawned below him. About the only thing, he said, that you can be sure of when you ask him for the grounds of his beliefs is that the reasons he gives you are not the real ones.

On August 1, we reached Chefoo. Mr. Swift and Mr. Trescot had arrived on the "Richmond." It was thought best that I should go on in advance to Peking and arrange for our negotiations, while my colleagues and my family remained in Chefoo. The Admiral took me on the "Richmond" to Taku, as far as a vessel with her draught could go. The "Ashuelot" then took me to Tientsin, where we arrived on August 3.

The next day at 4 P.M., accompanied by Mr. Holcomb, Secretary of Legation, and

six naval officers, I went to call on the
Viceroy Li Hung Chang, at his residence.
He received us very cordially and frequently
took occasion to express his friendship for
the United States. He was very anxious
to know why General Grant had not been
nominated again in June. I mentioned
three reasons, one of which was that there
was a strong feeling against a third term.
This he could not understand, repeatedly
affirming that a man who had served twice
was thereby better fitted for the place.

On the following day Li came with a large
retinue to the "Ashuelot" to return my call.
He remained an hour and a half and seemed
in fine spirits. He talked on several subjects
and joked freely. He repeated a remark
which I had made to him on the previous
day that the Brazilians who were trying
to make a treaty to secure coolies should
make a draft on us who were trying to
restrict the immigration. He told me in a
whisper that although the complications
with Russia on the Kuldja question were
serious, he believed China would escape
war. He said the idiots at Peking had
dreadfully blundered, that Tso (the Chinese
general in Kuldja) was a braggart, and that
he was now under strict orders not to pro-
voke war with the Russians.

[137]

Much to my gratification, Li had brought
General Gordon with him. The General
had come to China to persuade the government to keep out of a war with Russia.
He was living by himself in a Buddhist
temple, and I was told that he remained at
his devotions until ten o'clock, so that before that hour he refused all callers. Having heard of his military achievements, I
had fancied him to be a big English "swash-
buckler." Judge of my surprise when a
man of small stature, with a low and sweet
voice, with a manner almost feminine in
delicacy, quietly seated himself close to me
and told me his story. He said he had come
to persuade China to refrain from war, from
wasting her money on ironclads, the organization of a great army on the European
plan, and from a foreign debt. He said
that the true defence for them is howitzers,
fleet ships and a sort of guerilla warfare.
Their soldiers need no tents, and no com-
missary department. The way for them to
fight the Russians is to attack them at night,
allowing them no sleep, and then hasten
away till the next night. They can thus
keep them on the run and tire them out.
He tells them their capital is too near
Siberia and too near the sea. It can always
be easily captured. He was there with the

British forces in 1858–60, and knows the region thoroughly. He besought me to impress these ideas of peace on Li, as I had opportunity. He had come to meet me for the purpose of making this request.

The British government soon recalled him, because, it was reported, they were afraid Russia would take offense at his action.

Li invited me to dine with him on my return from Peking and placed at my disposal his steam launch to take me twenty-five miles up the river.

I availed myself of his offer, and after leaving the launch went by houseboats, drawn by men to Tungcho and thence by canal to Peking. Mr. Seward, the minister, received me at the Legation, and in due time introduced me to the Tsung-li-Yamen, and presented his recall. Prince Kung impressed me as far superior to the other members of the Foreign Office. They returned my call, and as they were passing through the drawing room, some one struck the keys of the piano. They hastened with a child-like curiosity to look in under the cover of the instrument to ascertain what caused the sound. Prince Kung announced the appointment of two commissioners to negotiate with us and assured me they would proceed with despatch.

The European ministers generally were in expectation of war with Russia. Under the walls of the city the soldiers were preparing by practice to meet the Russian army. This practice consisted of firing at a target with bows and arrows.

The Tsung-li-Yamen having learned that the Brazilian ministers were approaching to make a treaty, asked the American Secretary where Brazil was, and if it was a country of much consequence.

Having in two weeks completed my business in Peking, I returned to Chefoo. My colleagues and I and our families at once set out for Tientsin in the gunboats " Monocacy " and " Ashuelot." We exchanged calls with Li and hurried on to Peking.

On the journey up the river I had an interesting conversation with Mr. Trescot, concerning an event in the Civil War. After this lapse of time, I think I may be allowed to report it. In the American Case for the Geneva Arbitration of the so-called Alabama Claims, I had read that the British government, through Lord Lyons, the British Minister at Washington, invited our government to sign the Declaration of Paris (of 1856), and informed the Confederate government of this action. At the same time they invited the Confederate government to sign the second and third Articles and to omit the first, which forbids privateering, but did not inform our government of this action. Moreover, they sent the message to Richmond and Charleston, through Lord Lyons. If this plan had succeeded the South could have commissioned privateers, while we should have been precluded, and the carrying trade for both belligerents would have been secured to Great Britain. This was so dishonourable a trick, that I had always been reluctant to believe it. As Mr. Trescot was employed in our State Department at the time, and was also very familiar with transactions in the South, I ventured to express my doubts of the accuracy of the statement in the American Case. He replied, "You may well believe it, for I myself took the despatch from Lord Lyons to Richmond."

At the first meeting of the Commissioners with the Tsung-li-Yamen, we were informed that two Commissioners had been appointed to negotiate with us, Pao Chun, an aged member of the body with an excellent reputation for honesty, and Li Hung Tsao, one of the most noted historical scholars.

It will be understood that I held two Commissions, one as Minister Plenipotentiary and one as Commissioner to negotiate treaties. Therefore I had in hand the regular business of the Legation as well as work on the Treaties.

When we American Commissioners met to draft a paper to present to the Chinese Commissioner, there was a sharp difference of opinion between Mr. Swift on the one side and Mr. Trescot and myself on the other. Mr. Swift wished that we should demand the absolute prohibition of the immigration of labourers. Mr. Trescot and I maintained that we should ask merely for a stipulation giving us power to regulate, but not to forbid, absolutely, immigration. Mr. Swift asked that we telegraph to Mr. Evarts for authority to present his demand. We declined to do so. Mr. Swift of course yielded, but not without some feeling. We allowed him to spread on the record his propositions and his protest against ours.

When we read our statement to the Chinese, Pao said there were some difficulties on both sides, but he thought there were none which might not be adjusted.

After two or three meetings the details of which I will not give, we found one day to our surprise the whole Yamen in attendance. They had brought a full *projet* for a treaty, containing provisions that any restriction in immigration should apply to

California alone, that artisans should not
be excluded, that there should be no punishment for labourers coming in violation of the
treaty, and allowing persons, not Americans,
to import and employ Chinese labourers.
We did not encourage them to suppose we
could accept their draft, but took it away
for consideration.

Two days later we had a most anxious,
and, as it proved, a decisive session with the
Chinese. We took up the first Article in
their draft and the first in ours, regulating
immigration, and found ourselves so at vari-
ance with them, that Mr. Swift declared
they did not mean to give us a treaty, and
Mr. Trescot, usually hopeful, thought we
had come to the end, and that we had better
state our ultimatum and go. But I saw
the Chinese earnestly discussing and I suggested patience, saying that we might well
spend an hour there, that perhaps never
would our time be more valuable. Let us
leave this Article, I advised, and take up the
last. Let the fish chew the bait awhile.
The last Article was one which provided
that no laws we should pass in respect to
immigration should be operative until approved by them. This was so unreason-
able that they soon said they would waive
that. Then we took up the Article in

which they seemed to us to ask that Chinese
students and merchants could take with
them employees. They explained that they
meant by that only household servants.
To that we had no objection. Having now
got into the mood of agreeing, we went
back to Article I. I pointed out to them
that this clause asking that no limitation
should be excessively great or excessively
long was inappropriate to a treaty, and
would only cause discussion instead of
hindering it. They consented to change
that. As to their clause about penalties
they said they only wished to guard against
personal abuse and maltreatment. We
agreed to guard against this. We thus paved
the way for dove-tailing their first Article
and ours together, and the work was done.
It was agreed that Mr. Holcombe, the
Secretary, should come the next day and
with them arrange the texts.

Greatly relieved, we were about to leave,
when Pao detained us. He said he wished
to speak of one thing more. When the
Chinese treaties with the Western Powers
were made, they were one-sided. Now as
they wished to push new trade abroad, they
desired to secure equal commercial privileges. As the United States had always
been their friend, they preferred to begin

with us, and they wished to know if we could consider a proposition for a treaty or an article in this treaty on that point. We cordially responded that we would take the matter into friendly and sympathetic consideration.

Apparently the Chinese intended to give us the treaty we had made, but to concede us as little as possible. We completed the final agreement on the Immigration Treaty at 3 P.M., November 8.

We then left with them our draft of a Commercial Treaty. In it the two nations agree to favour the extension of commerce with each other, to fix the rate of tonnage dues and import duties on the same scale for both nations, to prohibit the trade in opium between them, and to provide for the trial of a person in the court of his nationality. We had reason to believe that the dues and duties for Chinese vessels entering Chinese ports were less than for our vessels. The request for the opium Article originated with Li Hung Chang. We were very willing to adopt it, though Mr. Trescot had fears that we might be criticized for it as we had no instructions on the subject. But I believed that it would meet with favour at home, though it might be criticized in England.

After the agreement on the treaties, the Chinese Commissioners sent presents to us, consisting of ham, sausages, fruits, chestnuts, and cakes for which the messengers, bringing them, expected and received suitable fees.

There was an interesting incident connected with the signing of the treaties. We had fixed on a day for signing them. When we arrived at the Yamen, the Commissioners with an air of great mortification announced that they could not sign on that day, that it was the Emperor's birthday, on which they could sign no document containing a word of unhappy significance, that such a word occurred in the treaties, and that in making the appointment they had not remembered that it was the Emperor's birthday, and they therefore asked for another date for the signing. Of course we assented, and on November 17 we all signed.

The European ministers were astonished when we informed them that after forty-eight days of negotiations, we had secured two treaties. On my arrival at Peking, Mr. Von Brandt, the German Minister, perhaps the ablest foreign representative there, told me that after two years of labour he had just procured a treaty and that I must not hope to finish a negotiation under a year. I have always supposed that whatever influence Sir Robert Hart had with the Chinese authorities was used to our advantage. I saw no evidence that any of the foreign powers made any effort to hinder us, though reports to the effect that some of them did were more or less current. My personal relations with all the Ministers were most cordial.

One of the most serious embarrassments of the Commission was due to what must be considered an error of the State Department in appointing my colleagues Commissioners Plenipotentiary, instead of Envoys or Ministers Extraordinary. The former title was unknown to our naval officers and to European diplomats. So there was trouble with the naval officers in respect to salutes and it required great care to avoid unpleasant complications in the social relations at Peking.

After the departure of my colleagues on the Commission in the early winter, my duties were those of the Minister. A few incidents may be worthy of mention, especially as illustrating the good disposition of the Tsung-li-Yamen.

As each village holds certain religious festivals annually, under Chinese usage, every village was taxed to meet the expenses of the festivals. The Christian converts were embarrassed by this requirement, as some of the features of the ceremonies were incompatible with the Christian faith. The Roman Catholics had some years before my coming procured the exemption of their converts from assessments for the festivals. When I learned this, I asked for the exemption of the Protestant Christians. The request was received with great courtesy, and soon an Imperial Decree was issued, relieving the Protestant natives from the assessment.

At an auction sale of the goods of a Presbyterian missionary who was about to leave Peking for America on a visit, some rude fellows in the crowd which an auction always attracts there, threw missiles into the grounds, broke down shrubbery, and caused much disturbance. When the news reached me that the disturbance was going on and threatening to become more serious, I sent a message to the Yamen, asking for protection to the mission. They at once sent a detachment of soldiers and arrested the mischief makers, and when I went to the mission on the next morning, I saw two or three of the men arrested, sitting in the street by the gateway of the mission, with

cangues on their necks. The authorities
offered to furnish an armed escort for the
missionary on his journey out of the city,
but I declined this as unnecessary. The
local official who should have prevented
the disorder was at once discharged, and
he appealed to me to interpose for his re-
appointment. Our local authorities have
not always been so efficient in protecting
Chinamen in our cities.

When Mr. Blaine was Secretary of State,
a rumour reached him that the Chinese
government was cherishing a plan to seize
the Hawaiian Islands. He sent me a very
spirited despatch, instructing me to call the
attention of the Yamen to this report and
warn them that our government would not
permit such an act. No one in Peking
attached any importance to the rumour. I
presented Mr. Blaine's statement with all
seriousness. It was difficult to make Chinese ministers comprehend the gist of my
inquiry about their intention to acquire the
Islands. But when they did, they burst
into a roar of laughter, and begged me to
inform the Secretary that whenever they
formed such a plan they would give the
United States timely notice.

The Japanese Minister, Mr. Shishido,
who had more than once confided to me his

[149]

troubles in doing business with the Chinese government, one day came to me, apparently much depressed in spirits, and said that he wished in confidence to lodge a document with me. The Yamen, he said, had made a treaty with him, and when the day on which they had agreed to sign it arrived, they refused to sign. He had, therefore, in indignation decided to leave for home. He had drawn a paper reciting the facts, which he was not showing to the other foreign ministers. But his nation felt so grateful to the United States for its kindness and especially to General Grant for his wise counsels to them on his recent visit, that he wished to leave this document in our hands.

I received it with hearty appreciation of the friendship evinced for us, and especially for the gratitude expressed for General Grant. I had learned so much in Japan and China of the great service Grant had tendered to both nations, that this tribute to him touched me with pride. He had warned them to keep out of war, especially with each other. He had showed them how war would put them in bondage to European creditors and how they should unite to effect a permanent co-operation in taking their places among the great self-reliant

powers of the world. I had come to feel
that his services to those two nations were
second in value only to his services to his
own nation. They both expressed to him
their desire that he would act as arbiter in
settling their trouble about the ownership
of the Loo Choo Islands. He declined, telling them, as he often did, that he was now
only a private citizen, and could take no
office. That fact they all came to understand.

Naturally I hastened to describe the action of the Japanese Minister to the State
Department, calling special attention to
what he said of General Grant. To my
great surprise, in due time I received a
reply from the Secretary of State calling
my attention in very serious tone to the
fact that General Grant held no official
post when he was in the East, and that I
should not have neglected my opportunity
to make that known. Why the honour
paid to General Grant should have gratified
the Secretary so little, I leave to the reader
to conjecture.

I was interested in finding that some of
the members of the Tsung-li-Yamen were
as keen reasoners in a discussion as one will
meet anywhere. Their intellectual training had been purely linguistic. The ques-

tion often suggested itself to me, whether this fact had any bearing on the discussions we so often have as to the value of our old classical training in preparing men for public life. These keen reasoners were almost absolutely devoid of mathematical or scientific education. I sometimes doubted whether in reaching their conclusions they were aware as we are of taking certain logical steps. If they were, they did not make known the steps to us, but at once stated their conclusions. There was only one man in the Tsung-li-Yamen who in discussion with me gave his grounds, one, two, three, for his opinion as we do. Much to my delight he and I worked so harmoniously that they left him to do most of the business with me. His mind seemed to me to work like the mind of a Western man — by logical processes.

One of the most interesting members of the Tsung-li-Yamen was the General Tso Tsung Tang, of whom Li Hung Chang had spoken to me as a boaster. Perhaps he was, but he was entertaining. He talked at my table of his campaigns in Kuldja with the dramatic air of a Frenchman. It was reported that he was appointed to the Foreign Office in accordance with a shrewd Chinese custom of curing a critic by giving him responsibility. It was related that when he came back from his campaign to Peking, he complained to the authorities that too great privileges were extended to the foreign legations, particularly that the French legation were allowed by the Yamen to enclose too large a part of the street in their yard. He was at once appointed as a member of the Board. It soon appeared that he enjoyed the society of us foreigners, who listened with interest to his conversation, and that no one cherished a more liberal spirit to us than he did.

When the Russian Czar was assassinated, he inquired who killed him. When told that it was the deed of Nihilists, he asked who they were. When informed that they were a secret society, pledged to kill sovereigns, he said, "Secret societies! they ought to make short work with them. A few years ago the province of Fuhkien was honeycombed with secret societies, and in their conflicts with each other they were destroying villages. The government sent me down there to restore peace. In about six weeks I had perfect tranquillity."

"Well, your Excellency," he was asked, "how did you accomplish that?" "Why, in two weeks I cut off the heads of about three thousand men, and it was perfectly quiet after that." And he spoke of it as calmly as though he were talking of killing so many flies.

A business meeting with the Yamen was always, in theory, a social meeting. Refreshments were invariably served, and it was vain to attempt to engage their attention to a matter of business until the refreshments were disposed of. It would seem that this usage was calculated to bring men to their conference in an amicable frame.

Sir Thomas Wade, the British Minister, was a most genial gentleman, with a large fund of Irish wit. As his family were in England during our residence in Peking, he was kind enough to be much in our house and contributed immensely to our pleasure. He had a great fund of stories. One he told on D'Israeli and Gladstone is perhaps worth repeating. D'Israeli once said to a friend in conversation that the English artists lacked imagination. Within an hour he had occasion to address a society of English painters and declared that they excelled in imaginative powers. Gladstone being told of this said he could see how in the fervour of debate one might say such a thing, but how one could do it in such circumstances he could not see. "It is hellish," he exclaimed.

[154]

Sir Thomas was a superior Chinese scholar. He wrote the text book which most students used in learning the language, and was fond of talking about the language. He said there is great difficulty in reducing the grammar to our categories. The Chinese do not seek classification of parts of speech but are content to follow precedent and usage. Exactness is attainable in the expression of thought in it, though its machinery for mode and tense is clumsy. It has changed but little in five thousand years.

It is sometimes remarked in diplomatic circles that a minister may become in a measure disqualified for his duties by too long service at one post. He comes to look at questions from the point of view of the people with whom he has long dwelt. It was charged that Sir Thomas often instinctively took the Chinaman's view of a controversy between England and China, and so failed to satisfy the British Foreign Office.

I have heard that once when President Grant was asked to appoint as our minister at Peking a gentleman who had spent most of his life in China, he replied that he had but one objection, namely, that he did not wish to appoint a Chinaman.

My intimate acquaintance with Sir Robert Hart, the head of the Imperial Customs, was of great help to me and the source of great pleasure. He, like Sir Thomas, was of Irish birth. He was a graduate of the University of Belfast, and a fine classical scholar. He kept up his reading of Greek and Latin in the midst of all his official cares. He was, of course, a great Chinese scholar. His advice to the government was supposed to be of great weight, as it deserved to be.

He told me, however, that one of his chief obstacles was the conservatism and stupidity of some of the mandarins with whom he had to do. For his diversion he played on the violin. He said that some of the mandarins declared that he was paid a large salary for sitting all day on his divan and fiddling.

The government had founded a college for the training of young Chinese to enter into the diplomatic service. The American missionary, Rev. Dr. Martin, was the President. During his temporary absence, Mr. Hart was put in charge. He asked me to visit the college from time to time and report to him what I found. The Professors were Europeans, who were teaching English, French, and Russian and branches of Western learning. They told me that the students were so afraid of being supposed to have any connection with foreigners, that they would not recognize them on the streets. The students were granted an allowance like our students at Annapolis and West Point. Mr. Hart wittily described them as the sons of mandarins who allowed their offspring for a consideration to be defiled with the pitch of Western learning.

Mr. Hart told me that he came near joining the Tai-pings in their great rebellion in 1859, and that he believed they would have succeeded if the foreigners had not joined the government in opposing them and that they would probably have given as good a government as that which prevailed.

He placed great stress on the filial respect and reverence of the Chinese, saying Providence had fulfilled the divine promise of length of days to the nation which obeyed the command to honour the fathers.

He talked frankly to me of some of their serious faults and of their antipathy to foreigners, and as if foreseeing what actually befell his own house in the Boxer troubles, said "None of us know how soon in some excitement our houses may all be in flames."

The most brilliant minister at Peking was Von Brandt, the German. He was the son of General Von Brandt, distinguished in the war of German Independence against Napoleon. He had served several years in Japan, and understood the Oriental mind thoroughly, and had the means of getting access to the secrets of the Chinese government. As the legations acted together on matters of common interest, he was of great service to us. His diplomatic career was terminated in a very romantic manner. He chose to marry a very accomplished American lady. At that time, it was not permitted to German diplomats to marry ladies not of their own nationality.

Two young men whose names afterwards became widely known were at that time in the German legation. One was Count Tattenbach, a member of a very old Bavarian family, who won distinction by representing his country in the Morocco troubles and also by being Governor of Alsace-Lorraine. The other was Baron Von Ketteler, whose bravery in attempting to leave Peking in the Boxer troubles caused his murder on the principal street of the city, at the spot now marked by an imposing monument erected by the Chinese government.

Although I had found my diplomatic labours attractive in many respects, and should perhaps have been disposed to continue in the service if ministers could have counted on a permanent tenure, I decided to return to my academic duties and therefore asked the President to accept my resignation.

On October 4, we bade adieu to Peking. A considerable number of our diplomatic and missionary friends gathered at our residence to say good-bye, and several rode out a few miles with us on our road to Tungcho. The life at Peking in our time was so remote from the rest of the world that the friendships formed there were very close. It was not without deep emotion that we parted from those whose society had been so dear to us.

On arriving at Tientsin, I called on the Viceroy, Li Hung Chang. He received me most affably, and thanked me very warmly for my part in making the Opium Treaty. I thought the opportunity favourable for telling him some plain truth. I ventured to say that I thought that he could carry England for the anti-opium doctrine in five years on one condition, namely, that the Chinese officials should in at least five provinces take hold of the work of suppressing the growth of the poppy with vigour. I assured him that the English maintain

that the Chinese wish to stop the importing
of opium merely to raise it themselves and
tax it for revenue. I do not think he enjoyed my remarks. He assured me that
in five provinces (Chi-li being one) the
growth was already controlled. It was not
courteous for me to question his statement;
but there was abundant evidence that
much was growing in Chi-li at that
moment.

I expressed the regret of my government
at the recall of the Chinese students from
America, which had just taken place. He
appeared also to regret it.

He courteously expressed the desire that
I should return to my post.

I attended the opening of a hospital
under very interesting circumstances. Miss
Howard, a medical missionary, who had
graduated at the University of Michigan,
had been assigned to duty at Tientsin. She
was called to render professional services to
the wife of the Viceroy, and had been the
means of restoring her to health. To show
his gratitude the Viceroy made a generous
contribution to found a hospital and induced his subordinate officials to contribute
also. On its completion Miss Howard fixed
a day for the opening, when I could be present and make an address. The Viceroy and

other high Chinese officials and the foreign
Consuls were present. The Viceroy made
very kind and complimentary remarks
about Miss Howard. In my address I of
course made proper recognition of his generous interest in the hospital. It has been
of great service to sufferers. I was told
that one man had brought his father in his
arms two hundred miles to be operated on
there.

In this connection I may say that in my
residence in China I was much interested
in the work of the Christian missionaries,
both Roman Catholic and Protestant.

Some of the Jesuit missionaries who
wielded so great an influence at the court
of the Emperors in the seventeenth century, were men of large mould as scholars,
divines, and statesmen. It was with great
reverence that I stood in the cemetery, just
outside the walls of Peking, where Ricci,
Schaal, Verbiest, and others lie buried, and
thought how near, as it seems to me, they
came to making China a Roman Catholic
country. For a time they won the favour
of Emperors, and led scholars and high
officials to adopt their faith. Their achievements, their lives of self-denial, their suffer-
ings form a most interesting chapter in the
history of missionary effort.

12

Unhappily the success which seemed coming to them was checked by dissensions which sprang up between them and the Dominicans concerning the lawfulness of ancestral worship for Christian converts. The controversy divided for a time the church in Europe and resulted in the condemnation of the Jesuits' position by two Popes and in a decree by the Chinese Emperor expelling missionaries from the land.

All missionaries who have prohibited those usages which we call ancestral worship have found that prohibition one of the gravest obstacles to the acceptance of the Christian faith. These early Jesuits, after a careful study, concluded that the usages were not properly called worship, but were only a manifestation of filial regard for ancestors, which was not at all inconsistent with Christian faith. Some of our modern Protestant missionaries hold the same opinion, though most of them do not. And Popes Clement XI and Benedict XIV were led to forbid it by Papal Bulls. The conflict on the subject raged in the Roman Catholic Church for three quarters of a century.

The presence of many American Protestant missionaries in China raised questions for my official action from time to time, as their work was interfered with by lawless men. But for the most part our missionaries showed much tact and judgment in avoiding difficulties. They called on me for help so much more rarely than some of the British missionaries called on Sir Thomas Wade that he once asked me jocosely if I would not trade missionaries with him.

Quite apart from any consideration of their religious activity, the influence our missionaries have exerted in preparing the way for the great change now going on in China can hardly be overestimated. A considerable number of the young men just sent to this country for education have received their training in the missionary schools. Each missionary station has furnished an illustration of the western learning they are coveting.

We spent a few days at Shanghai, awaiting the sailing of the French steamer Irawadi, for Europe. Dining one evening with Mr. Cameron, the manager of the Hong Kong and Shanghai Bank, he mentioned two facts worth repeating. He said his Bank had loaned many thousand pounds to Chinese merchants without taking so much as a scrap of paper to show for it, and the Bank never lost a sixpence by them.

Again, speaking of the testing of the silver sycee, in which they had to deal largely, he said they had in their service a Chinaman who by his mere sense of touch could determine so exactly the quality of the metal, that his finding in respect to it could be as absolutely relied on as analysis. It was apparently a gift inherited in some families.

I met at Shanghai an American of whom I had often heard, the freight agent of the China Merchants' Steamship Company. I was told that he had marked success in organizing the business, that he was very musical and that he was well versed in European languages. He was a coloured man and came to China with Anson Burlingame.

On our passage to Hong Kong the tail of a typhoon struck us astern and we were obliged to put on full steam to prevent the following waves from overrunning us. Chinese junks going north were lying with large baskets attached to their bows, slowly drifting astern. I asked the captain what was to happen if, in plunging on at such a rate, we came on one of these junks. "Ah!" said he, "nous le couperons comme un fromage." And I fear he cared as little as though the junk had been a cheese.

The voyage to Europe, thirty-eight days

from Shanghai to Marseilles, was very enjoyable. We called at Hong Kong, Saigon, Singapore, Point de Galle, Colombo, Aden, Suez, Port Said, and Naples. We had intended to debark at Naples, but were prevented by the fact that at Singapore we received some Dutch passengers from Java, where the cholera was raging. At Marseilles we were kept in quarantine twenty-four hours.

We made a tour through Italy, Germany, and Paris to London, and sailed from Liverpool on the Cunard steamer " Catalonia " on January 28, for New York.

I will mention here one incident on the journey, and our experience on the voyage.

Travelling by rail from Marseilles to Rome, we reached the little town of Ventimiglia in the early evening in the midst of what seemed to be a cloudburst. The train came to a standstill just before we arrived at the station, and remained there until the water, coming down from the cliff, reached the body of the cars. The officials of the road asked us to allow ourselves to be carried to the station on the backs of men. As I saw one fall down with a passenger, I declined and said we would pass the night in the comfortable carriage we were occupying. After a little the officials returned saying there was danger that the track and the station would be washed away, that the train would be pulled up to the station, and that we must leave the carriage. Accordingly we did so. We found the water on the station floor ankle deep. We made our way to a little inn. On entering we saw a horse hitched to the post of the front stairway. The barn had been undermined by the storm and the horse had been rescued. The innkeeper built a fire at which we dried our clothes and then went to bed.

The next morning I was told that the railway could not be repaired for some days. I decided to hire a coachman to drive me down the beautiful Cornice road to Genoa. Hardly had we started when the Mayor stopped us, saying that a building in front of which we had to pass was beginning to fall, and that the motion of our carriage might tumble it down altogether. I finally persuaded him to let us dismount and send the carriage past the building very gently, while we followed on foot. In this way we escaped from Ventimiglia.

We drove to San Remo to pass the night. As I was giving the coachman orders to call for us in the morning, I was informed that the railway bridge a few miles further on had been carried away and could not be

repaired for some days. After remaining
three days at San Remo, I learned that a
temporary footbridge had been erected
near Taggia by the side of the wrecked railway bridge, and that from Taggia trains
were running eastward. So we drove to
the footbridge, had our trunks carried over
by porters, and finally reached a train.
So much for railway travelling under the
shadow of the Italian Alps.

As the Cunard line of steamers had the
reputation of being very safe, I took passage
for my family and myself in the Catalonia, which had made but one voyage.
She was very commodious; but it proved
that her engines were not powerful enough
to hold her head up against heavy gales.
Unluckily we encountered three. She was
obliged to run before the wind in each case,
and so went far out of her course. The sea
broke into the dining-hall and flooded it.
As we approached Newfoundland the captain found we were getting short of fuel and
turned towards St. Johns to procure coal.
But we ran into so strong drift ice that this
plan had to be abandoned, and we had to
take our chance of getting to Halifax.
Another terrific gale delayed us. We ran
by the entrance to Halifax harbour and
barely escaped getting aground in a small

bay.   It was reported that we had to burn
some of the woodwork of the ship to make
the harbour.   Some of us resolved to take
the train to Boston.   But a three days'
snow storm had blocked the railway.   So
we remained on the ship and completed our
voyage to New York in nineteen days from
Liverpool.   The Company sent her back
without taking passengers.

We arrived at Ann Arbor on February 24,
1882, and received a most hearty welcome
from Faculties and students.

VII

THE CANADIAN FISHERIES COM-
MISSION AND THE DEEP WATER-
WAYS COMMISSION

In October, 1887, I was invited by President Cleveland to serve on an International Commission to adjust the difficulties which had arisen between us and Canada in respect to the fisheries in the waters near the eastern coast of Canada. More or less trouble had been experienced almost ever since the Treaty of Independence. It had often become serious since the negotiation of the Treaty of 1818, by which our privileges were greatly curtailed. Laws, which had seriously embarrassed our fishermen, had been enacted by Nova Scotia and New Brunswick, and later by the Dominion Parliament, and they had been administered with unfriendly severity, and, as we thought, in violation of the Treaty of 1818. The temporary relief furnished by the Treaty of 1854, and a part of the Treaty of 1871, was lost by the abrogation by us of the provisions which afforded the relief. The friction between our fishermen and the

Canadian authorities had become a menace to the continuance of friendly relations between us and our neighbour. Congress had gone so far as to authorize the President to execute retaliatory laws of a severe nature. They declined to authorize a commission to negotiate on the subject. There was hot blood on both sides.

In the early autumn of 1887, correspondence with the British government led the President to hope that an international commission might reach a peaceful and satisfactory settlement of the controversy by amending the Treaty of 1818 or by making a new treaty. The two governments agreed to submit the problem to such a commission. The British government appointed Joseph Chamberlain, Sir Charles Tupper, the Premier of Canada, and Lord Sackville West, the British Minister at Washington, as Commissioners. President Cleveland appointed Hon. Thomas F. Bayard, the Secretary of State, Hon. William L. Putnam, who had been for some time the counsel of our government in the fishery cases, and myself. I was led to accept, partly by the urgent request of Hon. E. J. Phelps, our Minister to Great Britain, through whose hands the correspondence of our government with Lord Salisbury had passed.

Lord Playfair told me he himself would probably have been appointed on the Commission if Iddesleigh had lived.

Some of my friends among the Republican Senators soon made it clear to me that we should take up our work under the heavy handicap caused by the fact that the President paid no regard to their recorded opposition to the appointment of a Commission. As usual, however, he followed his own judgment.

The Commissioners held their meetings at the State Department. Mr. John Bassett Moore, then Assistant Secretary of State, was our Secretary, and Mr. Henry Bergne, of the British Foreign Office, was the British Secretary. We held meetings two or three times a week, from November 21 to February 15, except for a few days at New Year's, when Mr. Chamberlain and Sir Charles went to Ottawa to confer with the authorities there. I shall not dwell on the details of our prolonged discussions.

From the very outset we were much embarrassed by a misunderstanding on the part of the British Commissioners concerning the scope of the conference. They claimed that we were met to consider the fisheries only as a part of our commercial relations, including in fact the tariff. If this were not understood to be the case, neither Great Britain nor Canada, they said, would be represented here. Although Mr. Bayard read his correspondence with Lord Salisbury in refutation of this assumption, and showed them that Congress alone could change the tariff, more than once, when hard pressed in argument on the details of our work, they returned to this statement, and with much apparent feeling. Our constant aim was to hold them to the consideration of the indisputable fact that much of the Canadian legislation concerning our fishermen had been of an unfriendly and unjustifiable stringency, if not in direct violation of the Treaty of 1818, and that some change in their policy was absolutely essential to the continuance of peaceful relations between Canada and us.

We finally presented a draft of a treaty which provided for delimitation of the exclusion from the common fisheries and for a liberal and just interpretation of the conditions, under which, by the Treaty of 1818, the "four purposes" for which fishing vessels were to be admitted to Canadian ports could be made available to us. It secured the free navigation by our vessels of the Strait of Canso, the purchase of supplies on the homeward voyage, and the liberty to unload and sell cargoes of fish from ships in distress. It stipulated that if duties on fish should hereafter be removed by us, the purchase of bait and fishing tackle, the transshipment of cargo and the shipping of crews, should be allowed by the Canadians. After prolonged discussions, in which on several occasions it appeared that we were at a deadlock and that no agreement could be reached, an agreement was reached on substantially the above provisions on February 14, 1888, and on February 15 the treaty was signed.

As the fishing season was soon to begin, the British Commissioners offered in behalf of Canada a *modus vivendi* for two years, by which on receiving a license an American fishing vessel could have the privileges accorded by the treaty, even though ratification of it had not been secured. This was presented in a separate communication to our government after the treaty was signed. The Treaty was soon ratified both by the Canadian government and by the Queen. But in our Senate it was opposed by every Republican and so failed of ratification.

The *modus* has continually been renewed by the Canadians: therefore in a sense we have been living under the Treaty. And no better proof of the worth of the Treaty could be asked for than is found in the fact that not for years previous had there been so little friction on the Canadian coast as there has been since 1888.[1]

The fate of the Treaty in the Senate confirms the belief that it is unwise to submit an important treaty for approval to that body when a Presidential election is at hand. A party in power is reluctant to have its opponent get the credit of settling a long and bitter controversy on the eve of an election.

During the winter I met many interesting men, of some of whom I may say a few words. I prize especially the acquaintance and friendship I formed with Mr. Bayard. A man of singular personal charm, I have never known one in public life of higher and nobler sense of public duty. He scorned the mean arts of the mere politician and whatever was unworthy in the spirit and policy of his own party. He was so magnanimous to his opponent, that to a certain degree his generosity unfitted him to ne-

[1] Since while the *modus vivendi*, which practically put the treaty stipulations largely in operation, continued in force, we had hardly any difficulties in Canadian waters, perhaps the writer may be pardoned for raising the question whether if we had ratified the Treaty, subsequent negotiations at least on the issues then under consideration, would not have been unnecessary.

gotiate with so keen a man as Chamberlain.
He was tempted to concede too much. He
was gifted with wit which was never un-
generous or bitter, but always most enjoyable. Perhaps I may be permitted to give
an illustration. Lord Sackville West, during our three month's discussions, never said
anything except to move to adjourn. In
reply to my inquiry, if in his official relations
with the Secretary he ever volunteered any
remarks, Mr. Bayard said, "No, he simply
communicates to me in writing a message
from Lord Salisbury, and acknowledges in
writing my reply. That is all." And then
he added, "I can hardly understand why the
British government keeps a minister on a
salary of $25,000, and then reduces him to
the function of a postage stamp."

I saw not a little of President Cleveland.
I was impressed with the readiness with
which he apprehended all the bearings of
the discussions which we reported to him,
and the promptness and soundness of his
conclusions. I remember being in his office
once at midnight, when he had a great pile
of papers before him. He said he must go
through them all before he slept. His
capacity for work was prodigious.

In company with Mr. Putnam, I saw
much of the Judges of the Supreme Court,

with all of whom he had an intimate acquaintance. Two good stories I heard at dinner at Judge Gray's are worth recording. One Judge Gray told of the English Judge Jessel. He had a very loquacious barrister before him one day. When the latter was pouring out a flood of words, the Judge asked, "Have you been before any other court with this argument?" "Yes," he replied, "but the Judge stopped me." "He did," said the Judge, "how did he do it?"

William Allen Butler, who was at the table, told of a judge who complained of insomnia. He said he had been unable of late to sleep on the bench.

Mr. Chamberlain displayed his well-known acuteness in discussion, but in repeatedly affirming that Mr. Bayard had given ground to suppose that we were to consider general commercial relations, in spite of Mr. Bayard's assertions and proofs to the contrary, he pushed his remarks to the verge of discourtesy.

Sir Charles Tupper, with bluntness defending the unjustifiable Canadian procedures, often found himself without any apparent disturbance by his inconsistencies in advocating measures one day which he opposed on the next day. In his fervour of debate he could not conceal the fact, though he often denied it, that his great aim was to compel us to remove the duty on fish so that his countrymen might have access to our markets.

The British Commissioners, after the completion of the Treaty, wished us to take up with them the Alaska boundary and the Behring Sea questions. We were not prepared to do so, and therefore declined.

On the initiative of Senator William F. Vilas of Wisconsin, on March 2, 1895, an Act was passed by Congress authorizing the President to appoint three Commissioners to confer with Commissioners to be appointed by Canada or Great Britain concerning the feasibility of the construction of canals which would enable vessels engaged in ocean commerce to pass from the Great Lakes to the Atlantic Ocean.

On November 4, President Cleveland announced the appointment as Commissioners of myself, as chairman, Hon. John E. Russell, of Leicester, Massachusetts, a former member of Congress and Lyman E. Cooley, C.E., of Chicago, Illinois, an engineer of high repute. The Dominion of Canada appointed as its Commissioners, Oliver A. Howland, M.P.P., of Toronto, Thomas C. Keefer, C.E., of Ottawa, and

Thomas Monro, C.E., of Coteau Landing. The last two were engineers who had long been in the service of the Dominion government.

On January 15, 1896, the American Commissioners took the occasion of the annual meeting of the Lake Carriers' Association to hold its first meeting in Detroit. We took a large amount of testimony from shipowners, masters, and merchants, who were much interested in our work.

On January 18, we held a joint meeting in Detroit with the Canadian Commissioners and marked out as far as was possible the plan which we proposed to pursue. We afterwards held another joint meeting at Niagara Falls, Ontario. The Canadian Commissioners co-operated with us most heartily there and afterwards, and furnished us from the public offices at Ottawa a large amount of valuable material, and made some special surveys to assist us.

As the problems to be studied were largely problems of engineering, Mr. Cooley was authorized to establish an office in Chicago and secure competent assistants to gather from all available sources the data required and prepare maps and plans. As only $10,000 were appropriated for the expenses of the Commission, we could not make special surveys, but merely collate and study the information which could be gathered from various sources, and draw our conclusions. This work of course fell mainly on Mr. Cooley, who proved most competent.

The investigation proved to the Commissioners of deep interest and, in their opinion, of great importance. It convinced us of the practicability of establishing deep-water communication between the Great Lakes and the Atlantic, and of the immense value to our nation and to the world of accomplishing the task. Whoever reads the interesting report prepared for us by Mr. Russell and examines the facts set forth by Mr. Cooley in his Exhibits, appended to the Report, will, I think, be also convinced.

President Cleveland transmitted the Report to Congress with warm commendations and recommended further appropriations for the continuance of the work. The Report with accompanying documents was published by the Government in 1897. But as no appropriations were made, the Commissioners proceeded no further. Perhaps the task may be taken up after the Panama Canal is finished. If so, the work of our Commission may prove of service.

VIII

SUMMER TRIPS TO EUROPE

On two occasions I have spent the summer vacation in Europe, chiefly in England. In 1886, my wife and I went abroad, with the purpose of dividing the summer between London and the cathedral towns. In 1891, Mr. Hazard and I went to London as delegates to the first Pan-Congregational Council, and afterwards went to the Baths at Wildungen in Waldeck, and to the Wagner Festival at Bayreuth.

What I am about to write is rather in confirmation of what Henry James said to me in London in reply to my inquiry how he found so great a charm in the life of that city. His answer was that the charm lies in the fact that there one sees so much life. "In Paris," he remarked, "one finds clever men within their limits. Here one sees more of many men and of very marked character."

Though in both visits I was in London only six weeks, and in midsummer, and in no official capacity, I met or heard discourses from a good number of interesting

men. This was in part due to the fact that
the American Minister, Edward J. Phelps,
and his wife were intimate friends of my
wife and myself and were in London in 1886.

At their hospitable table we met Robert
Browning. He was a short, rather stout
man with a cheery face, and was very
simple and cordial in manner. However
obscure is some of his writing, he was lucid
and animated in conversation. He said
his living in Italy was due to the delicate
health of his wife. He spoke at some
length of the stammering public speech of
Englishmen, which he thought was due to
an excessive consciousness and pride. He
said when he was a boy, speeches were common at ordinary dinner parties. He himself had a great aversion to making a speech.
He gave an interesting anecdote of the
effect once of inability to make a speech.
A motion was pending in the House of
Lords to alter the old law, which for-
bade a person charged with murder to have
counsel, and so compelled him to defend
himself. A venerable peer attempted to
advocate allowing such a man to have counsel. He found himself at a loss for words.
He could not go on. "You see, my Lords,"
he said, "my condition. Although I know
you are all indulgent to me, you observe I

am embarrassed to express myself. Suppose now I were on trial for murder. Any innocent man accused of that crime might be in my plight." The situation was so impressive that his view prevailed.

In answer to our urgent request that he come to our country and meet his many admirers, he gave no encouragement, though he expressed a most grateful appreciation of the favour shown to his works in the United States.

One of the most interesting men I met at the Pan-Congregational Council was Rev. John Brown, D.D., Pastor of the Church of Bedford, in which Bunyan preached, and author of an excellent biography of Bunyan. With him we visited Bunyan's cottage at Elstow. He informed me that Bunyan's family had lived in that village for centuries. He said he knew descendants of Bunyan more than fifty years old, who had never read "Pilgrim's Progress."

Dr. Brown told some stories of the wit of Dr. Magee, the Archbishop of York. Among them were these two. A man, with whom he was discussing, said, "I am not so stupid as I may look." To which the Archbishop replied, "For that give God thanks." When he went to York to be consecrated as Archbishop, some woman passing by him,

exclaimed, "What an ugly mouth!" He.
overhearing it, said to her, "You are right,
madam, but it has made my fortune."

Dr. Brown and other preachers spoke
freely of the social disadvantages under
which young men and young women in
dissenters' families found themselves. He
informed me that one Anglican clergyman
in his neighbourhood had recently in a
sermon or public address declared that
persons married by any but an Anglican
clergyman were living in adultery. When
Dr. Brown called the attention of the
clergyman's bishop to this the clergyman
was reprimanded.

At a tea given by the Bible Society at
their house, I saw what was said to be the
largest collection of Bibles in the world,
and was told the following story of the
origin of that renowned society:

A Welsh girl, named Mary Jones, walked
many miles to beg a Bible of a minister.
He had none to spare for her. She went
home weeping, but on his promise to get
one for her, she walked again twenty-five
miles to procure it. The minister came to
London, told the story, and persuaded men
to found the society.

I went one morning at 8 o'clock to breakfast with the directors of the Tract So-

ciety at their rooms in Paternoster Row. These directors, busy men, fifteen in number, meet every Tuesday morning at that early hour for breakfast and the transaction of the business of the society. They were criticizing tracts which they had all carefully read. Here, as at the meeting of the directors of the Bible Society, I was deeply impressed by the fidelity of these officers of the societies in the discharge of their duties.

Calling at the Foreign Office on Mr. Henry (afterwards Sir Henry) Bergne who was the English Secretary to the Fisheries Commission on which I served in 1887–8, I was introduced to Sir Edward Herstlet, and was shown by him into the rooms where the Treaties are preserved. I seemed to have a large part of the history of modern Europe in my hands as I held an Official copy of the great Treaty of Vienna of 1815 and one of the Treaty of Paris of 1856.

As an illustration of the remark of Henry James about the life in London, I may say that attending one afternoon a garden party given by Lord and Lady Jersey, I met and was presented to, among others, Mr. and Mrs. Lecky, Lord Sherbrooke, Sir Richard Webster, then Attorney General, now Lord Chief Justice, Prof. Ray Lankester, and Mr. Knowles, editor of the *Nineteenth Century Magazine*. On the return in the train, an English gentleman, speaking of the peerage just granted to Bass, the brewer, repeated Labouchere's quotation concerning the elevation of Allsop, "*Surgit quidquid amarum.*"

Mr. Ouless, the painter, told a good story in my hearing. Poole, the fashionable tailor, having lent money to some of the nobility, was sometimes invited by them into company. Once, when he had been to Lord ——'s, he was asked what he thought of the gathering. He replied that it was well enough, but the company was a little mixed. "How," some one said. "What could you ask? You could not expect they would all be tailors."

Perhaps the most striking illustration of freedom of speech in England is witnessed in Hyde Park on Sunday afternoon, when the advocates of every opinion are allowed such unrestrained liberty of utterance in the hearing of any persons they can induce to listen. At various stands on one occasion I heard the following speakers. No. 1: A Spiritualist; No. 2: An atheist; No. 3: Anti-government, anti-rent, anti-everything existing, a French revolutionist in manner and in appearance; No. 4: A lay preacher

[185]

of the gospel. No. 5: A reformed drunkard; No. 6: An anti-vivisectionist; No. 7: A rabid and radical socialist. The spiritualist and the lay preacher had the largest audiences. But the authorities interfered with none of them. There was no disorder.

In 1891, Mr. Hazard and I made a visit to the Continent after the close of the Council in London. We spent some days in Brussels, where Mr. Hazard had important business relations. I asked prominent men there why Belgium, a neutralized country, charged itself with the expense of an army of a hundred thousand men. Their answer was that the Great Powers virtually require it to prevent any state from taking advantage of a defenceless condition, and furthermore, the officers drawn from the higher classes have influence enough in the government to maintain an effective force.

We spent some time at Wildungen in Waldeck, where are excellent springs with medicinal qualities like the waters at Carlsbad. The waters, however, are cold and most palatable. Some five thousand visitors, mostly German, were there, among them being our friend Carl Schurz. These springs apparently are not widely known in this country, though they deserve to be. From this little state came Bunsen, the historian, Kaulbach, the painter, and Rauch and Drake, the sculptors. I took long walks into the surrounding country, which is inhabited by well-to-do peasants. They have comfortable houses, but the manure heap, apparently the accumulation of months, is often in the front yard. Sometimes the residence is in the second story, the barn occupying the first story.

We went to Bayreuth to attend the Wagner Festival. Knowing that Jean Paul lived in that town for years and died there, I sought to find his house. The cabman had no knowledge where it was. Entering the principal bookshop, I asked a young woman who was in charge, where the house was. She was unable to tell me. Soon strolling down the street, not fifty rods from the bookshop, I came on the house, a fine three-story dwelling with an inscription on it, giving me the information I desired. Verily, I thought, the prophet was without honour in his own country. We found his statue and the grave of Liszt without inquiry.

IX

THE MISSION TO THE OTTOMAN EMPIRE

In the spring of 1897, I was asked by Rev. Dr. Storrs, President of the American Board of Commissioners of Foreign Missions, if I would accept the position of Minister to Japan or Turkey, if desired by the President. Mr. William E. Dodge, of New York, speaking for the Presbyterians, asked the same question with respect to Turkey. They both had in mind the interests of Christian missions. I gave both to understand that if the offer of such a position came unsought by me, I would give it consideration.

In April, Senator McMillan, at the request of President McKinley, inquired by telegraph whether I would accept the position in Turkey. After some correspondence, I finally wrote that I would accept, provided I could return at the end of a year or remain longer if I chose. While, with my wife and daughter, I was on a visit to New Orleans, my name was sent to the Senate and promptly confirmed. On my return home the Regents gave me leave of absence for a year from October. The Legislature of Michigan passed a vote of thanks to the President for the appointment.

On May 6, I visited Washington and had interviews with the President, Secretary of State John Sherman, and other officers of the State Department, all of whom received me very cordially. But two despatches were received from Mr. Terrell, our minister at Constantinople, which led me to ask the President to excuse me from serving. The first said the report had come to him that while in the South I had charged Russia with fomenting disturbances in Turkey, and that on this account my relations with the Russian Ambassador would be strained. The second stated that the Sultan objected to me because I, like most of the American missionaries, belonged to the denomination of Congregationalists. I did not desire to go with these difficulties as a handicap. But Secretary Sherman telegraphed my denial of the truth of the first despatch. It being soon ascertained that the Sultan had made the mistake of confounding the denomination of Congregationalists with such an organization as the Congregation of the Jesuits, with which he had controversies, our Secretary in charge of the Legation telegraphed that the objection to me was withdrawn.

I may as well say here that no one of the European Ambassadors was more cordial to me on my arrival than Mr. Nelidoff, the veteran Russian Ambassador and that the other ambassadors in answer to my inquiries, assured me that they never heard the least criticism of me from Mr. Nelidoff, or from any Embassy or Legation.

Furthermore, I may say, that the Sultan was always most affable to me in my interviews with him, even when I had to discuss some missionary questions. In fact, I never saw any traces of the difficulties which Mr. Terrell reported.

The President and the Secretary declined to listen to my requests to be excused from service. I decided to go to my post, and made my arrangements to sail on July 17, for Havre. My wife and I left home on July 14. We reached Paris at an early hour on July 26. While we were there, floods in Austria destroyed the railways, by which we had planned to go to Constantinople. So we were compelled to go to Marseilles and take the steamer.

On the way south we visited Avignon, Nîmes and Arles. After a comfortable voy-

age on the Messageries steamship "Senegal,"
we reached Constantinople late in the afternoon of the 18th. Mr. Riddle, the Secretary, Mr. Short, the Consul, and a Turkish
official, representing the Grand Vizier, were
at the wharf to greet us. In the Legation
launch we proceeded at once to Therapia
and took lodgings for the summer at the
Palace Summer Hotel. The next morning a
messenger from the Sultan called to greet me.

As soon as convenient I made my calls
on the Ambassadors and Ministers. Baron
Calice, the Austrian, was the Dean, a most
courteous and amiable man with an English wife. His long service at that post
made his knowledge of affairs valuable to
us all. Nelidoff, the Russian, soon transferred to Rome, had been considered the
most influential representative. He was
succeeded by Zinovieff, a shrewd man, whose
whole career had been made in Asiatic
service. He informed me that Russia
trained its men in diplomatic service,
especially for Asiatic or for European posts.
He had been much in Persia and understood the operations of the Oriental mind.
Russia treats Turkey as belonging to the
Asiatic department.

Sir Philip Currie, the British Ambassador, had been taken, as Pauncefote was,

directly from the Foreign Office for diplomatic service. He was a man of the finest presence; but he could not get on with the Sultan. His English love of justice and honesty made him impatient with the artful devices and the wickedness of the Turkish officials. He was obliged to see Great Britain losing its influence and could not conceal his indignation at the policies of the Turkish government. But it was refreshing to hear his noble English spirit express itself.

Lady Currie, known in her own country as an author of fiction, was a woman of great brightness of mind and of singular charm of manner.

Monsieur Cambon, the French Ambassador, was a most attractive personality. He had been at his post in the time of the massacres and exerted himself to the utmost to induce his government to interpose by force to put an end to the cruel violence. He thought the Great Powers missed a rare opportunity at that crisis. He had the finest powers of a French conversationalist. I always counted it a happy hour when I could meet him. He is most worthily representing his country in London. He is an elder brother of the ambassador who won such favour with us at Washington

[192]

during the Spanish War, in the delicate position of being the medium of communication between us and Spain, and who now holds the difficult position of French Ambassador at Berlin.

The German Ambassador on my arrival was Baron Saurmar-Jeltsch, who had been Minister at Washington, a large, bluff, blue-eyed hunter, who liked killing wild boars better than formal dinners. But he was soon succeeded by that able and distinguished statesman, Marschall von Biberstein, a man of high intelligence and great force of character. The German Emperor, who has sought and not without success to secure the influence in Turkey once wielded by Great Britain, sent this strong and vigilant man to carry out his policy. He soon made his power felt, and until the deposition of the Sultan, Abdul Hamid, was undoubtedly the leading ambassador at Constantinople.

Signor Pansa, the Italian Ambassador, was a very agreeable gentleman, but Italy apparently did not find her voice considered of as much weight as that of the other Great Powers.

My relation with the Spanish Minister, Urrutia, was very friendly. He was transferred after a few months and succeeded by a Marquis, who had been at St. Petersburg. In that capital, as is well known, social functions begin at a very late hour, sometimes at midnight. He was asked after he had been in Constantinople some weeks, how he found life there. "Oh," said he, "in many respects very well. But I must say it is the dullest place I have been in, after 2 o'clock in the morning." He was a most affable gentleman, and although the outbreak of the Spanish War compelled him and me to break off formal social relations, we never sacrificed our friendly feelings.

At the time of my arrival the ambassadors of the six Great Powers were in session with an Ottoman representative for the purpose of adjusting the relations of Turkey with Greece and the Balkan States. The Congress did not accomplish very important results. The diplomatic wits said it served to show "*l'impuissance des Grandes Puissances.*" But in part at least owing to their influence a satisfactory Treaty of Peace between Turkey and Greece was negotiated.

It is well known that German officers, loaned to the Sultan by the German Emperor, really planned the campaign against Greece nominally conducted by Edhem

Pasha. One of the German officers who was wounded in the war told me that the Turkish victories might easily have been made more decisive if the German advisers could have persuaded the Turkish commander to get up and have any fighting before noon.

On September 3, I was received by the Sultan. The whole staff of the Legation and the Consulate, were present. Court carriages came for us. The Assistant Introducer, Ghabit Bey, who had called on me in the name of the Sultan, on my arrival, occupied the carriage with me and my dragoman. The soldiers at all the guard houses saluted as we passed. Arriving at the Imperial Palace, the Yildiz Kiosk, Munir Pasha, the Chamberlain, met us. Officers in brilliant uniform were gathered in the large reception room. The Secretary of Foreign Affairs, Tewfik Pasha, then escorted me to a smaller room, where the Sultan was standing by the side of a small table. He wore his semi-military blue frock coat with no binding and wore many jewels and decorations. I read my speech in English, of which one copy in English and one in French had already been sent. The Turkish Secretary then read a Turkish version. The Sultan replied in a low but pleasant voice, substantially reciprocating the wishes and sentiments I had expressed. The Secretary also in a gentle tone rendered the Sultan's speech in French. The bearing of the Sultan was affable and cordial.

I then withdrew to the salon, where cigarettes and light refreshments were served. The great hero of the Russo-Turkish War, Osman Pasha, and other notable persons were present. After a little we returned to the Legation and served refreshments to the guests.

On the next day I made my calls on the Ministers of the Porte. I will say a few words of those with whom I had subsequently to do business.

The Grand Vizier, Khalil Rifaat Pasha, was an old man whose mind seemed to act very slowly, but who in all my dealings with him was just and fair and obliging.

The Secretary of Foreign Affairs, Tewfik Pasha, was a most affable and attractive man. I sometimes thought he was too ready to agree with me and to say yes to my requests, especially when it proved he had not the power to make good his promises. He had been Ambassador at Berlin, and there married a German lady. I often wondered whether in accepting his hand she supposed she was to be admitted to diplomatic society in Constantinople. As a matter of fact she was obliged, like all Turkish wives, to live in seclusion.

Zahdi Pasha, the Minister of Public Instruction, was an amiable elderly man with whom I had much pleasant conversation on education. He regretted the failure of many officials to appreciate the value of general education. He complained that this greatly hindered his work, in which he seemed deeply interested. I may relate an incident which illustrates the devoutness of the pious Turks, which they are not ashamed to have us know. On calling at his office one day at 3 o'clock, I saw him kneeling and praying. I proposed to the porter that I should withdraw until he was free to see me. "Oh no," said he, "come in and take a seat." I did so. The Minister on his prayer rug continued some ten minutes at his devotions, then arose, and without any ceremony greeted me and gave attention to my business. One could hardly have such an experience with a cabinet officer in a Christian land.

He rendered me a valuable service in instituting a search for an ancient manuscript, alleged by the author of a book, written in Missouri, to be in the library of

Santa Sophia. This book is entitled the "Archko Volume." It professes to give the contents of manuscripts called the Acta Pilati, found in the Vatican, and confirmed in the library of Santa Sophia, giving many details concerning the early life and the trial and execution of Jesus. It was published in Philadelphia by the Antiquarian Book Company in 1896. It bears on the face of it the appearance of a fraud. A gentleman sent me the book with the request that I ascertain whether there is in the library of Santa Sophia such a manuscript or book as is referred to by the author as the authority for the narrations he gives. The Minister informed me that the library in question was under his special care and he would order a most thorough search. A few weeks later he informed me that the search had been made and that there was no trace of any such work in the library. His report did not surprise me.

Said Pasha, President of the Council, had been formerly Secretary of Foreign Affairs and Ambassador to Berlin, and had been in public service all his life. He was a fine story teller and had a good sense of humour. He spoke with much interest of John A. Kasson, who represented us at Berlin. Among his stories was one of his handling of a missionary case when he was Governor at Salonica. An American woman teaching a missionary school had been annoyed by a young Turkish hoodlum throwing stones at her school house and made complaint to the Governor. He summoned the lad and was satisfied of his guilt. He then sent for the young woman, told her that he desired to frighten the fellow by threatening him in her presence with very severe punishment, and suggested that if she would then interpose and ask for his release the effect on the public would be most salutary, and insure her and her colleagues against further annoyance. She had the good sense to agree to this treatment of the case. His programme was carried out and there was no further interference with missionary work while he was in Salonica.

Of all the ministers, he and Tewfik Pasha alone spoke French. Munir Pasha, the Sultan's interpreter, spoke French. It was generally believed that the Sultan, who when a lad was some time in Paris, could understand it fairly. But he insisted in using Turkish altogether in his interviews with the diplomats.

The Porte under Abdul Hamid had lost the power which it had under his predecessors. He insisted on reviewing the whole of their work before action was taken on any affair of the least consequence. Therefore after working for weeks to carry a measure through the Cabinet, the foreign representative found his work only just begun. And even with the best purpose on the part of the Sultan to expedite business, it was simply impossible for him to accomplish it. And if he did wish to delay it, he had a ready excuse. The diplomatic body with one accord were greatly dissatisfied with the course which had to be taken, even with urgent business. Moreover there had grown up a sharp rivalry, one might almost say hostility, between the Porte and the Secretaries and other officials at the Palace. It was currently reported and widely believed that the Secretaries at the Palace had to be bribed if important measures were to be attended to with any promptness.

One day, after the completion of a little transaction which had dragged along for weeks, I said with some impatience to Tewfik Pasha, "Why do you have such ways of doing business? I have heard that you are cousins to the Chinese. And you do have this same habit of provoking delay in finishing a task which in America we should do in fifteen minutes. Why is it?" With his amiable smile, which partially disarmed me, he replied, "Well, I can only say that is our way." And that was the only explanation.

Of course I had several interviews with the Sultan on business. Although subsequently our Legation was raised to an Embassy on the alleged ground that the Minister had not the same facility of access to the Sultan which the Ambassadors enjoyed, I had no occasion to make that complaint. I found no difficulty in securing an audience when it was necessary. The bearing of the Sultan was always affable. He heard with attention what I had to say and replied politely. On one occasion, during an audience, a messenger entered in great excitement with what appeared to be an important message. I offered to withdraw. The Sultan detained me. He gave some orders to the messenger. He then informed me that the message was that his sister's palace on the Bosphorus was on fire and that he had given orders to have the firemen hasten to the palace and to have his sister and her children brought to his palace. Then he proceeded to preach a brief but excellent sermon to the effect that when misfortune comes we must do our best to avert it, but having done that in resigna-

tion and faith, must leave all to God. I
ventured to reply that his doctrine would
be deemed good in all lands.

He remarked playfully to me one day
that I was the only American Minister who
ever came to his court who spoke French.
In this I think he must have been in error.

When he learned that I was going to
Jerusalem and Damascus, without any request on my part he sent orders to his
officials in the Holy Land to greet me and
aid me in my journey. They did this to
an extent which was sometimes almost em-
barrassing. I mention his courtesies, because I cannot but criticize and condemn
many features of his government.

Though he was averse to allowing capital
punishment, it was believed that his morbid
fear of assassination and his dread of revolution led him to severe punishment of
mere boys and to the exile to remote provinces of some of the best men in the empire.
Two cases of the unjust punishment of boys
came to my personal knowledge. A lad
who had been a student in Robert College
found his funds exhausted so that he could
not complete his education there. Having
heard that the Sultan sometimes gave
scholarships in a Turkish school, one Friday
he pushed through the military lines which

guard the Sultan on his way to the mosque, and threw into the carriage a petition for the scholarship. It is a tradition of great antiquity in Oriental lands that any subject may petition the sovereign. When the lad came home, one of his comrades asked him how he succeeded in approaching the Sultan's carriage. The lad replied with fatal indiscretion, "Why, it was easy enough. I was so near him I could have shot him." This unhappy remark being repeated, he was arrested, charged with threatening the life of the Sultan, convicted and sentenced to fifteen years' imprisonment. All efforts of influential friends to secure a modification of the sentence were in vain.

The other case occurred in the Turkish Medical School in Constantinople. Some men of revolutionary spirit gained access to the school and scattered incendiary circulars about the building. One of these papers was found in the room of a young student from Smyrna, though he affirmed through no agency of his. He was banished, but his poor mother could not learn where. In her despair she made, through a lawyer whom I knew, a request of me that I would forward through the Sultan's Secretary a petition to His Majesty, that she might be informed where he had been sent, and that she might be allowed to go to the same place and see him occasionally. Finding that under the usages at the Palace I could without impropriety oblige her, I did forward the petition, which was one of the most pathetic papers I ever read. But I never heard of any results.

Many absurd laws and regulations in force in the capital at the time of my residence were believed to be due to the Sultan's fear. For instance, though the city had nearly a million inhabitants there was no local mail. One had to send letters by special messengers to persons in the city. It was said that though there had formerly been mail facilities, the Sultan suppressed them because he received so many threatening postal cards and because conspirators could by mail easily mature dangerous schemes.

I had two singular controversies with the customs officers to handle. An Englishman, after visiting the hospital connected with one of our American mission stations, generously sent out from London a thousand dollars' worth of medicines as a present for the physician to use in his merciful work. In the invoice was a small quantity of carbolic acid, a remedy used in the treatment of sore throats. It happens that it can

[204]

also be used in the preparation of the explosive gun cotton. On that account the whole shipment was stopped and threatened with confiscation. I laboured for some time with the officers, explaining to what an innocent and even beneficial use the dangerous article was to be put and urging them at least to seize that and sink it in the Bosphorus and let the rest of the medicines go on to their destination. Suddenly, as I thought I was on the point of success, the customs official, with whom I had been labouring, was succeeded by another. He took up the matter *de novo*. As though nothing had been said he sent me a note, informing me of the arrival of this shipment of medicines, saying the duty paid on it was so much, but that the fine on the acid was so much more, and he would thank me for a cheque for this excess and that the whole shipment had been confiscated. So I had to start all over again, and take as many more weeks to secure the release.

One comical case occurred. Robert College had appointed a young graduate of an American college to teach the Oriental boys not only some branch of book learning but also the American game of base ball. In examining his baggage, the custom officers came upon a pitcher's mask. "What

is this?" they asked themselves. "Some
new kind of revolutionary weapon?" They
detained it as a strangely suspected article.
After a week's deliberation and full explanation by the American consul it was permitted to enter.

The Sultan watched with much interest
the events of our war with Spain and
especially the naval contests. He asked
me many questions about them. Finally
he inquired if I could tell him how he could
procure some ships like ours without the
intervention of middle men, who were so
given to cheating him in contracts. I told
him that the builder of the "Oregon,"
which had performed its wonderful feat of
coming round Cape Horn and going directly into action, was then in St. Petersburg, and if he desired, I would ask him by
telegraph to come to Constantinople and
confer with him. I endeavoured to impress
him with the belief that very much of our
success depended on the man behind the
gun. His mind was evidently turned more
to our cannon than to our men. He said
he had ordered some of the cannon. It is
well known that he did finally order an
ironclad of the Cramps of Philadelphia.

In this connection I may mention a singular fact about the attitude of the middle-

class Turks towards us in the Spanish War.
The sympathies in most of the Embassies,
except the British, were rather against us,
though they were never manifested to me
in an unpleasant way. The newspapers
published in Constantinople, except one
edited by a Frenchman, were rather unfriendly to us. That one I kept well informed of our views. But rather to my
surprise I found that the main body of the
Turks in the capital leaned to our side. I
was puzzled to know why. Therefore I
asked a friend who was familiar with the
Turkish language and with many of the
people to ascertain the cause of their attitude. "Why," they said to him, "don't
you remember that three hundred years ago
these Spaniards drove the Mohammedans
out of their land? Allah is great. The time
of punishment for them has come." Not
improbably the Sultan shared their feelings.

At the outbreak of the war I asked him
if he proposed to publish a proclamation of
neutrality. He said he would follow the
example of other nations and that the Great
Powers guaranteed the neutrality of the
Dardanelles at all times. I asked how
about furnishing munitions. "Oh," he replied, "everyone knows we never spare so
much as a pistol."

It will be remembered that the Spaniards sent some ships of war as far as Port Said, on the way to Manila. They could not proceed farther without procuring coal. Tewfik Pasha asked me what international law required of his government about allowing the Spanish ships to coal. Of course I told him his duty was to allow them to take coal to return home but not to go on. The Spanish ships returned home. I have always supposed he knew the law without asking me. But I am not quite certain about it.

As I have spoken with emphasis of the dilatoriness of the Turkish government, I may properly credit them with commendable promptness in one case. During the war with Greece the lights on the Turkish coast were extinguished to prevent the Greek war ships from approaching. In December, 1897, after the close of the war, the United States gun-boat, the Bancroft, was coming from Athens into the port of Smyrna in the evening. The captain saw the outer light at the mouth of the harbour burning, and so concluded that the port was open at night and kept on his way. As he was passing a small fort on an island in the harbour, he was fired on by musketry without any notice. He stopped his engines and sent a boat with an officer towards the fort, and the boat was fired on. The Bancroft anchored till daylight and then proceeded into the harbour and reported to Admiral Selfridge, who was there with the war ships, the Brooklyn and the Olympia. The Admiral made his complaint to the governor, who referred him to Constantinople. He sent a despatch to me and with it one of the bullets which had fallen on the deck of the Bancroft.

I at once sent a spirited despatch to Tewfik Pasha, demanding an apology and the punishment of the officers of the fort at Smyrna. The Imperial Council met the next day and decided to meet all my demands and to dismiss the officers at fault. The Admiral expressed himself as satisfied, and the affair was ended.

Whether action would have been so prompt if our ships under Admiral Selfridge had not been lying at Smyrna I cannot say, but I doubt it. Unhappily perhaps for some other business in my hands, owing to the outbreak of the Spanish War the Olympia was just then sent through the Suez Canal to Manila, where she had a part in achieving Dewey's notable victory, and the Brooklyn was ordered home for duty on this side of the sea.

[209]

My belief is that if Selfridge could have remained at Smyrna with those vessels, our claims against the Turkish government would without great delay and without the firing of a gun have been settled. When I was asked to go to the East, largely for the purpose of procuring a settlement of our claims, with my knowledge of Oriental ways I asked, and the President promised, that the vessels should be ordered to the Turkish coast. These claims were chiefly for the destruction of the property of American missions by Turkish soldiers. As they were under the control of the government, and in a legal sense its agents, and the property for which restitution was asked was destroyed not by rioters but by them, the responsibility of the government could not be denied. In fact, when I presented this argument to Tewfik Pasha, the Secretary of Foreign Affairs, he did not and could not deny its validity. On the contrary, he told my dragoman that they would willingly settle our claims were it not for the embarrassment caused by the larger claims of the other nations. When the Great Powers were in conference they decided to present their claims not jointly but separately, in notes substantially identical. The various Ambassadors assured me that they

were quite willing I should present ours at
once and one of them said he should be very
glad if we succeeded in collecting without
delay. With the outbreak of the Spanish
War and the withdrawal of our vessels, the
Foreign Office relegated the question to the
limits of indefinite discussion and procras-
tination, which lasted beyond my term of
service. A settlement of the claims was
finally made after some years more of delay,
by adding the sum due to a contract price
for the construction of a ship of war by the
Cramps, this excess to be turned over by
the builders to the mission board whose
property had been destroyed.

The resort to espionage was a most serious blot upon the administration. The
spies of the Sultan were everywhere. One
Turk said to me the spy business was the
most prosperous of any. I was assured
that spies were sitting at the dinner tables
of the principal hotels, to overhear the conversation of the guests. With one against
whose visits I had been warned I had an
amusing adventure. He was a handsome,
dignified Arab, who had been in England
long enough to talk English fairly well.
He introduced himself to me, saying he had
been Mayor of Jerusalem and was now trying to procure from the government a con-

cession for the construction of a system of waterworks for that city. He regretted, he informed me, to find that the government was so corrupt that he had no hope of securing his concession except by bribing a whole row of high officials. It was refreshing to him to turn aside from these representatives of a corrupt and tyrannical government and pay his respects to the representative of a pure and honest democracy.

Supposing his object to be to draw from me some remark derogatory to the Sultan, which he could report to my disadvantage, I ventured to remark that a monarchy presided over by a just sovereign was an edifying spectacle and that even in republics there were found sometimes corrupt men in office. He seemed surprised at my remarks and proceeded to eulogize republican governments. I continued my commendations of enlightened monarchies. The conversation ran on in this way for half an hour, when he bade me adieu, but as I flattered myself without any game for his bag.

The venality of some of the courts was also a fearful weakness in the government. I asked one of the best lawyers, an Englishman who had been practising twenty years in Constantinople, whether the courts had improved in his time. "They have decidedly grown worse," was his reply. He then gave me the following illustration from his recent experience:

"I was counsel for a Liverpool merchant to collect a sum due him from an Armenian merchant here for a bill of goods. Not long after the trial began I saw evidence that one of the judges had been bribed by the defendants. I asked and procured his dismissal from the bench. Another man was appointed and the trial was resumed. After a little I ascertained that this man was bought up by the defendants. I arrested proceedings and asked for the removal of the new judge. Thereupon the Armenian came to me and offered to settle for half the face of the bill. "But why," asked my informant, "do you ask me to accept half the sum due? You know you owe the whole." "Oh, well," replied the merchant, "but it has cost me half the amount of the bill to buy these two judges."

Some of the religious ceremonies one sees in Constantinople are of much interest.

On January 9, we went to the Yildiz to see the Pilgrims start for Mecca with gifts. A Mohammedan acquires much merit by making the journey. The streets leading to the scene were lined with people. The concourse of women was exceptionally large. Dropped down on the grassy banks, wearing their white wraps, they resembled a flock of pigeons. As we looked on, a long procession of venerable ulemas poured forth from the mosque, where they had been to worship. They wore robes of every shade of green and a gilt band around the turban. The procession was headed by several camels and by a larger number of donkeys, laden with the gifts. Most of these gifts were covered by canopies of multi-coloured stuffs. But the last donkeys carried just such old hair-covered trunks as I used to see in the country in Rhode Island in my boyhood. As the procession started, a sham fight was carried on, representing an attack on the caravan, but a few brave Moslems successfully defended it. The old priests with much difficulty and considerable boosting mounted horses, each of which was led, and closed the procession. The day was perfect. The wild Arab music, the real or simulated enthusiasm of the defenders of the caravan, the gay trappings of the camels, the large concourse of the faithful, all made a fine Oriental pageant of semi-barbaric nature. It is however always well understood that the procession will not march overland to Mecca, but will be borne by steamer to Arabia.

On May 2, we attended the reception by the Sultan of the high religious and civic officials. This is held in the great hall of the Dolmar-batsche Palace. The diplomatic visitors, including the ladies, occupied the gallery. We were asked to be present at half-past six in the morning. The Sultan sacrifices a sheep but not in our presence. The ceremony began by the Sheik-ul-Islam approaching His Majesty and receiving a kiss on his shoulder. Then priests of high rank came forward and kissed the hem of the Sultan's coat. Those of lower rank kissed a tassel fastened to the Sultan by a gilt band and held by Osman Pasha. These and the civil officers all wore their official dress. The Sultan extended his hand a little as if to seem to lift up most of the priests from their bowing position. But in recognition of the salaams of the other officials he made not the slightest response by movement or gesture. A band played in the gallery during the whole ceremony. Tea, cakes, and fruits were served to us visitors during the long and rather monotonous ceremony. Munir Pasha, the Sultan's interpreter, came at the close to thank us.

I attended a remarkable and rather repulsive ceremony of the Persians at their

Khan. They are known as the Shiite branch of Mohammedans. They believe that Ali, the son-in-law of Mohammed, was crowded out of the caliphate by his rivals for years and his son Hassein was murdered by them. Annually they have this celebration in honour of Hassein. The excitement is so great on the occasion that not unfrequently scenes of violence are witnessed. On this account it was not deemed prudent for me to take my wife with me.

It was already dark when I arrived. The place was brilliantly lighted. Round and round the building in the centre of the square, which is bordered by houses and shops of Persians, the procession marched from sunset till about 10 o'clock. It consisted of three principal sections of about sixty or seventy persons in each. One was made up of men beating their breasts as they marched before what seemed to represent a turbeh or tomb of Hassein, and responsively shouting something about him. Another section carried chains with which they flagellated their bare shoulders. The third section carried swords. They were clad in white cotton gowns, and as they marched and shouted they cut their scalps and faces with their swords till their necks and gowns were saturated with blood. One child five years old, riding a horse, did the same, and I even saw an infant in arms with a knife and its face and head apparently slashed. This last section grew more and more excited as the evening wore on. From time to time men became so weak that they were led away to be washed and cared for. Near the close of the evening one man appeared to be raving crazy. There were musicians, flag bearers and light bearers in the procession.

I understand the demonstration to be one of grief for the death of Hassein and also of penance. Many of the Persian bystanders wept and some sobbed aloud. In the houses adjacent, groups of Persians were looking on in gravity. Some of them were weeping, some were partaking of refreshments.

The Turkish soldiers were present in force to keep order. One might well believe that otherwise these frantic zealots would run amuck on the Giaours present. I was told that in Persia the demonstrations on such an occasion were more violent.

My wife and I frequently visited the Institutions, of which Americans may justly feel proud — Robert College and the Woman's College. The former was established by that gifted missionary Cyrus Hamlin, endowed largely by Mr. Christopher Robert, of New York, and administered for so many years by Rev. Dr. George Washburn. It gave a good collegiate education of the American type to a large number of Armenian, Bulgarian and Greek students, and thus incidentally imbued them with the Christian spirit of regulated liberty. Several of the men most prominent in developing the civic life of Bulgaria were graduates of the college. Perhaps no foreigner in the Empire was so well informed about the political condition of South-eastern Europe as President Washburn. So highly was his opinion valued by the British government that he rarely passed through England without being asked by the Premier or the Foreign Secretary for an interview. A few Turkish students were in the college classes, but owing to the attitude of the Imperial authorities not many ventured to attend. English was the language of instruction in both colleges, though the eastern languages were taught.

The Woman's College had girls of the same nationalities as Robert College. Occasionally a Turkish girl was sent there by her parents. On one occasion I attended a class in English Literature. It happened that the subject on that day was Longfellow's "Evangeline." I was surprised at the command of our language by these Oriental girls, and especially by the fact that the most proficient was a Turkish girl, the daughter of a Turkish official in the Treasury Department. I was told that she had entertained her father in his leisure hours by translating at sight to him passages from Shakespeare and from Holmes' "Autocrat of the Breakfast Table." She had translated into Turkish an American book, "Abbott's Mother at Home," if I remember the title correctly, a work intended to instruct mothers in rearing their children, and her proud father had incurred the expense of printing it and distributing a thousand copies among the soldiers returning from the Greek War. It is an interesting fact that this Woman's College owes its imperial authorization to Admiral Farragut. It had long been asked for in vain. He was informed of this on his visit. When he was received by the Sultan, in the friendly conversation of their interview, he asked the Emperor to give the college the sanction of an irade and his request was granted.

The summer of 1898 we spent in the island of Prinkipo, in the spacious mansion of Mr. Azarian, and with our launch made many beautiful excursions to the adjacent islands and to the main land.

On July 4, we invited all the Americans in Constantinople and all the members of the British embassy. One of the British gun-boats was placed at the service of the Americans living on the Upper Bosphorus, so that our company numbered about sixty. We pinned little American flags on all, British and Americans indiscriminately, and had a merry celebration. Unhappily the news of the capture of Cervera's fleet did not reach us until the next day and even then was denied at the Spanish Legation.

One day we went to Bulwer's Island, some seven miles away from Prinkipo. It is named after Sir Henry Lytton Bulwer, who negotiated with us in 1850 the noted Clayton-Bulwer Treaty. He built here two castles of stone in Norman style. Earthquakes have made ruins of them, though one can see the elaborate carved decorations of the doorways and windows. It is said that his life here was of such a character as to lead to his recall and caused Lord Palmerston to give his successor the advice "Beware of Islands."

The adventure of an English neighbour of mine on Prinkipo is perhaps worth relating. Long resident in Constantinople, he had been an anonymous correspondent of a London newspaper, through which he made known to the public many facts concerning the Turkish government, which the Sultan preferred not to have proclaimed. The tidings came to my friend that the Sultan was preparing to banish him from the country. He had large interests in Constantinople which made it very undesirable for him to leave. He bethought himself of this device.

He sent for an influential Turkish official to whom he had once rendered an important service and who had promised to reciprocate the service if opportunity ever presented itself. He said to his friend, "I am thinking of going to England, and running for Parliament. I know of a district in which I can be elected." His friend besought him to remain, but immediately went away and spread the news among the officials at the Palace. They saw that in Parliament he could do much more harm than in Constantinople. Nothing more was heard of the scheme to banish him.

Since during the great fast of Ramazan it is impracticable to transact important business with the Turkish government, my wife and I left Constantinople on January

26, 1898, on my sixty days' leave for a journey to Egypt and the Holy Land. We went up the Nile to Philae, spent several days in Cairo, then went to Joppa and Jerusalem, to Jericho and Hebron, to Beirut, where we visited the American College as the guests of President Bliss, to Baalbec and Damascus, calling on the way home at Smyrna and making an excursion to Ephesus, finally reaching Constantinople on March 23. At every town which we visited in the Holy Land, the governors and military and civic officials, in obedience to the Sultan's orders, welcomed us on our arrival, and during our stay rendered us any assistance in their power.

One of the most agreeable excursions we made while in Turkey was to Broussa in fine days in May. The situation is most picturesque on heights from which one looks over a wide expanse of fertile valleys to the Sea of Marmora. Here Osman, the founder of the Empire, planted himself. Here are his tomb and the tombs of some of his successors. Here Pliny the younger was praetor, and here he wrote some of his letters which have come down to us. While we were there, a regiment which belonged to Broussa and the neighbourhood returned from the Greek War. The streets were crowded with men, women and children. We expected to hear the soldiers greeted with cheers. To our surprise, not a sound of a voice was heard. The march of these stalwart and sun-burned warriors, returning from a triumphant campaign, was made through the principal street in dead silence everywhere. I inquired what was the explanation of this strange scene. I was told that the government had never sent home or allowed to be sent home during the war any tidings concerning these men. Consequently the relatives were waiting in anxiety now to see who, if any, were missing. In this suspense there was no impulse to cheer. Those who were rejoiced to see their kindred returning were restrained from a public demonstration by a delicate regard for the feelings of those to whom the day brought disappointment and sorrow. This explanation made the spectacle very pathetic.

I had an interview with the Acting Governor-General Halib Ibrahim Bey. He had been Vali at Sivas at the time of the massacres and had been removed on the demand of the British Ambassador. But he now talked to me in the most liberal spirit of leaving freedom to all as far as possible. He sent the military commandant and his dragoman two miles out to meet me on my arrival and a squad of cavalry all the way to the sea on my return.

On August 5, I had my farewell audience with the Sultan. He talked mainly on our war with Spain, and asked me to request our Secretary of the Navy to commend to him some ship-building firms with whom he could deal directly. He thanked me for having maintained so cordial relations with him.

On August 13, we embarked on an Austrian steamer for Trieste. Some forty or fifty of our friends, missionaries, teachers, and diplomats gathered at the wharf to bid us adieu. Our Turkish coachman and servants evinced much feeling. It was not without emotion that we parted with our faithful servants and our numerous friends.

X

THE PRESIDENCY OF THE UNIVERSITY OF MICHIGAN

In 1869, to my surprise I was invited to visit the University of Michigan and decide whether I would accept the presidency of the institution which Dr. Haven had resigned. My wife accompanied me, and we spent two or three days at Ann Arbor. We were much impressed with the vigour and the promise of the University. But on returning to Burlington, I found that the men who had rallied generously to the support of the college would be sorely disappointed if I left them then. I decided that it was my duty to decline the invitation to Michigan. So I devoted myself with all my energy to the continuance of my work in Vermont. In 1871, the invitation to Michigan was renewed with much earnestness. I felt that I had discharged my duty to my Vermont friends and that the college could move on fairly without me. I had some hesitation about undertaking so large a responsibility as that at Michigan. One day when I mentioned this to a friend who had very large business interests, he said, "I have found if you have a long lever it is as easy to raise a large load as to lift a small weight with a short lever."

After careful consideration I decided to accept the invitation to Michigan. In compliance with the request of the Regents of the University, I attended the Commencement at Ann Arbor on June 28, 1871, and delivered my Inaugural. I then returned to Burlington and finished the academic year which terminated on August 3. I removed to Ann Arbor with my family early in September.

I found that largely under the influence of John D. Pierce, Superintendent of Public Instruction at the time of its organization, of Isaac E. Crary, and of Henry P. Tappan, its first President, the University had been inspired to a considerable extent by German ideals of education and was shaped under broader and more generous views of university life than most of the eastern colleges. Mr. Pierce, a graduate of Brown University in the class of 1822, was settled as a Presbyterian Home Missionary in Marshall. Mr. Isaac E. Crary, a graduate of Trinity College, Hartford, was a lawyer in the same town. Both were much interested in public education. Mr. Pierce was appointed the State Superintendent of Public Instruction, the first officer with that title in the United States. Mr. Crary was a member of the Convention that framed the State Constitution of 1835, and as Chairman of the Committee on Education drafted the Article on Education in the Constitution. Cousin's famous Report on Public Instruction in Prussia had fallen into the hands of Mr. Pierce and formed the subject of much discussion between him and his neighbour, Mr. Crary. Mr. Pierce told me that he could take me in a grove in Marshall to the very log on which they often sat and conferred together on this remarkable book, which gave them the idea of a state system of schools with a university at its head. That idea gave shape to the constitutional Article on Education and to the legislation afterwards enacted in accordance with it. When Dr. Tappan was made President in 1852, he brought from Germany, where he had studied, ideals quite in harmony with those which Pierce and Crary had cherished at the outset, and with his vigorous mind he left a deep impression on the life and spirit of the University. The Institution had in its Faculties at the time of my arrival men of marked ability. I will name some of the more prominent of the professors who are no longer living.

Dr. Henry S. Frieze, Professor of Latin, for the two years prior to my coming Acting President, was a man of rare qualities, a passionate lover of art and of music, a scholar of large and varied attainments and of the finest literary taste, an inspiring teacher and a most winsome spirit. His influence on students and on his colleagues, in fostering the love of classical learning and in the diffusion of high and broad university ideals through all the West, causes his memory to be cherished with peculiar respect and affection.

Rev. Dr. Benjamin F. Cocker, Professor of Philosophy, had had a romantic life. A Methodist circuit preacher in Yorkshire in early life, he lived for years among the miners in Australia. On his voyage from that country he was wrecked on an island in the Pacific, inhabited partly by savages. After a narrow escape with his family he arrived in this State in utter destitution. Assigned to the care of a small country church, his talent soon made him known and secured his call to important churches, and finally to the chair in the University. His opportunities for gaining an education had been slender, but by his marked ability and his great industry he had overcome in large degree the limitations of his earlier years, though he never ceased to lament them. Both as a preacher and a teacher he had a singular charm of voice and manner which, added to his clearness and simplicity in discussions of the problems of philosophy, made his instructions a delight to his pupils. He is remembered by them with abiding affection and gratitude.

Edward Olney, Professor of Mathematics, also had a unique history. He was never in school but a few weeks. Of mathematics he seemed to have from childhood an intuitive comprehension. His geometry he learned while following the plough. He drew the figures with chalk on the plough beam and mastered the demonstrations while travelling in the furrow. Though probably his attainments did not at last reach much beyond the range of the higher instruction in the undergraduate course, he had a most unusual gift as a teacher. He not only made his instruction simple and clear, but what is not common in colleges, he made the study of mathematics a favourite study of the great body of students. He had a manly frankness and honesty of character which often gave to his expressions the air of bluntness, but commanded the highest respect of his pupils and cultivated in them a spirit of manliness and honesty kindred to his own. He was a man of most earnest religious nature and was a power for righteousness both in college and in the community.

Charles Kendall Adams was Professor of History. He had acquired his enthusiasm for historical study under Andrew D. White, when he filled the Chair of History in this University. Mr. Adams had recently returned from study in Germany where he had become familiar with the *Seminar* method, in introducing which he afterwards was the pioneer in American universities. Mr. Adams was even then greatly interested in university problems and was carefully studying all experiments in university administration, both in America and Europe. He subsequently made good use of his knowledge of universities as President of Cornell University and of the University of Wisconsin.

Moses Coit Tyler was Professor of Rhetoric and English Literature. He was already master of that attractive style which lent such a charm to everything that he wrote and inspired his classes with a love for the best in literature and for purity and vivacity in their essays and speeches. In his private study he was already showing that deep interest in American History and the early American authors which gave shape and colour to his later works. He had a fine sense of humour which enlivened his instruction and made him a most agreeable companion.

Alexander Winchell, like Professors of Science in most American colleges at that time, was giving elementary instruction in Geology, Zoölogy, and Botany, but by his powerful imagination and brilliant eloquence was widely known as one of the most successful popular lecturers on science. He was afterwards President of the Syracuse University.

James C. Watson, Professor of Astronomy, was a man whose mathematical intuitions were near to genius. The son of an Irish carpenter, he was one of the finest products of the Michigan System of Public Education, for he received his entire training in the public schools of Ann Arbor and in the University. While he was yet a student he made a telescope and with it discovered a comet. While still a young man he discovered asteroids and wrote a text book on Astronomy, which gave him an enviable reputation among astronomers

[231]

here and in Europe. His college teachers said that as a student he was almost as apt in languages as in mathematics, and if he had cultivated them as a profession, might have won distinction in that field. He had unlimited capacity for work. It seemed as though he could observe all night and then study all day. In teaching he had none of the methods of the drill master. But his lecture or his talk was so stimulating that one could not but learn and love to learn by listening. I have heard his pupils say that sometimes while discussing an intricate problem he would have an entirely new demonstration suddenly flash upon his mind as by inspiration and then and there he would write it out upon the blackboard.

George S. Morris, a man of the widest reading, was the Professor of Modern Languages. He had already translated Ueberweg's History of Philosophy. He afterwards welcomed the opportunity to give his whole time to teaching philosophy here and in the Johns Hopkins University, leaving in both institutions a profound impression upon his classes.

Edward L. Walter was then giving instruction in Latin. Later he had charge of the work in German and in the Romance

Languages. He was a master alike of ancient and modern literatures. Gifted with remarkable powers of acquisition, he was one of the most successful of teachers. We were robbed of him while in the prime of his strength by the sinking of the steamship Bourgogne.

M. L. D'Ooge, Professor of Greek, was absent in Europe, but the department was in the hands of Elisha Jones and Albert H. Pattengill, than whom better classroom teachers of the classics were to be found in no American college.

In the Medical Department, which was crowded with over five hundred students, were Professor Corydon L. Ford, doubtless the best lecturer in the country on anatomy, as it was then taught; Dr. Sager, a man of large scientific attainments for his time; Dr. Palmer, so long the efficient Dean; Dr. Prescott, the distinguished chemist, and a group of brilliant younger men.

In the Law Department were the three great teachers, who had guided its fortunes from its foundation, Thomas M. Cooley, James V. Campbell, and Charles I. Walker. Never was a law school so fortunate as this was in beginning its work and continuing it for so many years under such gifted instructors. Charles A. Kent, a worthy

[233]

coadjutor, had recently joined them. It was not strange that the school attracted students from all parts of the land.

Professors Cooley and Campbell were on the Supreme Bench of the State. The Court, by the wisdom of its decisions, had already won the highest respect of the legal profession throughout the country. Judge Cooley had also won renown by his great work on Constitutional Limitations. He seemed to have an intuitive perception of legal relations. He was a man of indefatigable industry. Beyond all men I have known, he possessed the power of writing rapidly and with such accuracy that no reader could misunderstand his meaning.

Judge Campbell was a scholarly man of wide reading, and of a graceful style in writing or speaking. He was most familiar with the early history of the State and especially with the customs and traditions of the French population of Detroit and the vicinity. His narrations of the details of their life were as fascinating as those of the best French *raconteurs*. His lectures on law were diffuse, but so charming in manner, like his conversation, that they held the undivided attention of his students.

Professor Walker was so lucid and methodical in his instruction that his classes always testified to the great benefit they received from him.

It will be seen that it was rather remarkable that a University so young as this should have gathered such a company of teachers. It was indeed a stimulating body for me to be associated with in my arduous and responsible duties.

On my arrival I was sadly disappointed to find that my former teacher and old friend, Dr. Frieze, at whose suggestion I had been chosen President, had gone to Europe for a prolonged visit. I had relied on him to give me full information about the details of the Institution and to assist me with his wise counsels. But I received a warm welcome from the Faculties and the students. During the first few weeks, I attended classes to observe the methods and the quality of the teaching. I found the instruction was for the most part excellent. In both the colleges with which I had been connected, we had a marking system for recording the quality of the students' recitations. Here I found none. I was naturally interested to observe whether without such a system students could be held to a proper standard of work. When, after six weeks' attendance on classes, I heard only two students say "not prepared," I was forced to the conclusion that as good results were secured without as with a marking system. Prolonged observation in later years has confirmed that belief, although probably higher technical excellence in recitation is attained by a few who are studying for class rank. But the appeal to a college student to work for the sake of learning is an appeal of a noble sort, and if heartily responded to, yields a result of a higher order than an appeal to ambition for class rank.

I was early impressed with the great advantages both to teachers and students of having the three departments: the Collegiate, known here as the Literary, and the Medical and the Law Departments all upon the same ground. It gave a certain breadth and catholicity to the views of all. The professors, organized as a Senate, met socially at stated intervals to listen to papers and discuss them, and so to consider subjects from their different angles. As there were no dormitories, the students of the different departments were thrown together in their temporary homes and were led to see that there were things worth knowing outside of their own special lines of work.

I was also soon struck with the good results of the plan adopted the year before my arrival of bringing the High Schools into closer relations with the University, by receiving on diploma the graduates of schools which had been approved by the Literary Faculty after inspection of them. This innovation on the practice of American colleges was due to the fertile mind of Dr. Frieze, who took the idea from the usage of the German Universities in receiving the graduates of the Gymnasia without examination of the students. In adapting the plan to our needs, the Faculty wisely made provision for a visit to the schools by some University Professors. I made many of these visits. The advantages both to the schools and the University were soon obvious. The methods of the school visited and the fitness of the teachers for their work were made known to the visitors. The opportunity for suggesting improvements was furnished. Interviews with scholars were held. Frequently the visit was made the occasion for a public address on education to the citizens. Conferences were had with the school board. An opinion could be formed concerning the willingness or unwillingness of the town to give the needed support to the school, for the maintenance of the proper standard of school work. An impulse was given to the public to take a new interest in the school which the University thought worthy of a visit. Above all, an intimate and friendly relation between the school and the town on the one hand and the University on the other was established. The University was also enabled to see what was possible to the High School and was guarded against the danger of asking too much of the students as the condition of admission.

It was thought 'by some that the officers of the school would not be courageous or careful in maintaining high requirements for the graduation of students who were to go to the University. It proved that with few exceptions they were both courageous and careful and that sometimes they declined to recommend students to us who might have entered on examination by us. They had a better opportunity to know the qualifications of students by observing their whole school course than we had in a single examination, in which the pupil by diffidence or accident, might not do himself justice. After a few years of experimentation, we found that judging by the first year of college work the students received on certificate made a better showing than those received on examination. Perhaps in nothing has the University been more use-

ful to the educational system of the State
than in the cultivation of the friendly relation with the schools by the introduction
of the diploma system of admission of students. Our example in establishing it has
been generally followed in the West, and to
some extent in the East, though not always
with our precautions in making visits.

The year before I came, the doors of every
department of the University had, under
the pressure of public opinion in the State,
been thrown open to women. Most of the
professors and of the students would have
preferred that they should not be admitted.
On my arrival the subject of their admission was still under discussion. The objections raised were, first, that women could
not master the difficult studies of college,
and, secondly, that the health of women
would suffer under the strenuousness of
college life. Experience soon showed that
neither objection was well founded. As it
required some courage for women to come
at first, fortunately those who did present
themselves were generally earnest, self-
reliant, scholarly persons. By their dis-
cretion and their scholarship, they won the
respect of teachers and fellow students and
made the path easy for those who came
after them. A good number of them, after

graduation, obtained commanding positions in the Faculties of Women's Colleges, which were springing up in the East, and won honour for themselves and the University.

By way of illustration I may speak of our relation to Wellesley College. When Mr. Durant, the founder of that Institution, was making up his first Faculty, he encountered difficulty in finding women with suitable training for filling professorships, because there were so few colleges where women could receive the proper training. Naturally, he wrote to me to inquire whether we had been graduating such women as he needed. I recommended a graduate of the Class of 1874 for his Chair of History. She proved so satisfactory that he then wrote asking me to recommend thereafter any woman whom I should deem competent. That greatly delighted me, and I sent him one after another whom he promptly appointed. Among them finally was Alice Freeman who subsequently was appointed President and made so distinguished a career.

The collegiate education of women has proved of great value to the schools. Formerly they could not easily find opportunities for training which fitted them for the best work in the high schools. If by any

means they had obtained it, they did not
feel sure of it. They lacked the confidence
which is essential to the success of a teacher.
But when they had graduated in the same
classes with the most scholarly men who
were teaching, both they and the school
boards had confidence in their training.
The schools, in which a majority of the
teachers have always been women, took on
new vigour and life.

The fear that the joint education of the
sexes would lead to serious embarrassments
proved so unfounded that it is found almost
without exception in the Colleges and Universities of the West. It cannot be doubted
that the example of this University con-
duced largely to this result, and, judging
by our correspondence, was helpful in
opening the doors of some European Universities to women.

Our friends in the East have always
expressed surprise that most of the colleges and the universities in the West have
for the last thirty years educated the sexes
together. They fail to see that co-educa-
tion in those institutions was the natural
development of the plan followed in the
high schools of the West. Whereas in the
high schools of the East the sexes were
educated separately, in the West they were.

[241]

as a rule, educated together. Having thus been instructed together up to the very door of the college, it was no violent or unnatural transition for them to enter the college together. As in fact no serious objections to their joint education have presented themselves, the usage bids fair to be continued at least in the West.

As I have always been fond of teaching and have thought it was well for the President of a College or University to teach, I soon availed myself of the opportunity which presented itself to give some instruction in International Law and in Political Economy. I continued to do so until I went to China in 1880. On my return I resumed the work in International Law and continued it till I resigned the Presidency.

In order to keep in close touch with students, especially those of the Literary (Collegiate) Department, for several years I discharged the duties now assigned to a Dean. I registered all new comers; I granted (or refused) excuses for absence. I took the initiative in examining all cases for discipline. The result was that I knew every student and could call him by name up to the time of my departure for China in 1880. Of course it was easy for me to do this in Vermont. But it was more difficult when I had to do with eight hundred students. The influence and the pleasure it gave me was a great reward for the effort required. I wonder that the President even of a great University willingly foregoes the satisfaction which comes from such an intimate relation with even a portion of his students as comes from giving instruction in some subject.

In 1873, largely through the influence of Mr. Claudius B. Grant, at that time a Regent of the University and a Member of the Legislature, we persuaded the Legislature to give us the proceeds of a twentieth-mill tax. This established a most useful precedent. In later years our twentieth-mill tax was raised first to one-eighth, then to one-quarter, and then to three-eighths of a mill. This proved to be a far better plan than the voting of special appropriations for a number of objects. It spared the legislative committees and the whole Legislature the trouble of scrutinizing a large number of specific requests. It also enabled the University authorities to use the funds granted them more effectively and more economically. For frequently it happened that before the term of two years for which the appropriations were made had elapsed, it became apparent that the money granted for some particular object could be more wisely devoted to some other purpose. Furthermore it is quite essential to wise administration that the authorities of a University should be able to lay plans for some years ahead; and resting on a tax bill which experience shows is not likely to be repealed, they can adopt wise policies for the future, when they might not be able to do so if they had to depend on specific appropriations to be renewed at every session of the Legislature.

I had occasion to visit the Legislature at several sessions to make known to our Committees, and sometimes to the whole body, our needs, and several times the whole Legislature visited the University. I wish to bear witness to the courtesy with which I was always received at Lansing, and the hearty interest in the Institution which the members of the Legislature always evinced on their visits to us.

Eastern critics of the system of State support of universities have often assumed that the institutions would become embarrassed by being entangled in the controversies of party politics. It can be affirmed that such has never been the case in the support or control of this University. Different parties have been in control in this State during the life of the Institution. But we have fared equally well, whichever party was in power, and no political controversy in the Legislature or in the State at large has ever embarrassed us.

The example of our Legislature in passing a tax bill, providing in a lump for the needs of the University, has been followed by several states to the great benefit of their Universities.

In 1875, the Legislature made appropriations for the establishment of the Homeopathic Medical School, the College of Dental Surgery, the School of Mines and a Professorship of Architecture. These new departments of work were at once organized. Unhappily in 1877 the Legislature did not continue the appropriations for the School of Mines and the teaching of Architecture and we were obliged to drop the work. This illustrates the difficulty of administering a University which depends on biennial appropriations.

In 1879, under the pressure of urgent requests which I had made for some years, the Regents established the Chair of the Art and Science of Teaching, to aid in preparing our graduates to teach in our schools or to superintend schools. Our action was severely criticized for a time by some college

[245]

men who maintained that teaching could not be taught through formal instruction. But only a few years elapsed before nearly every university of standing, including those which had criticized us most severely, appointed Professors of Education or Pedagogy. As a consequence, so-called Schools of Education with large equipment have grown up in some of these institutions.

In the late seventies a large freedom in the election of studies in the Literary Department was granted; the course of study in the Medical Department was extended from two years of six months to two years of nine months, and the School of Pharmacy was organized. During the decade from 1870 to 1880, the progress of the University in all departments had been most satisfactory.

This was especially gratifying because from 1875 to 1879 an unpleasant controversy was raging which threatened havoc to the Institution. The accounts of the Chemical Laboratory showed a deficit for which the Director of the Laboratory or an Assistant Professor was apparently responsible. If the decision of the question of responsibility had been left to the Regents alone, it would probably have been soon settled. But for reasons which need not

be discussed here, persons outside of the
University became interested and a bitter
contest ensued, involving the Legislature,
the Courts and the Public. It is obvious
now that the difficulty was largely due at
the outset to the defects in the system of
bookkeeping in the Laboratory. It was adequate in the days when the number of students was small, but was not well suited to
meet our wants when the classes had become
very large. After the controversy was
ended, it gave way to a better system. It
is a good proof of the strong hold the University has on the respect and affections of
the people that the fierce and prolonged
contest left it unharmed.

During the last thirty years there has
been a constant and steady movement forward in the enlargement and enrichment of
the work in all the departments. The Engineering which was carried on as a part of
the Literary Department has been devel-
oped into a separate Department, compris-
ing Civil, Mechanical, Electrical, Chemical,
and Marine Engineering, in close relation
with Architecture and having nearly three
hundred more students than were found in
the entire University when I came here.
The introduction of the elective system into
the Literary Department added greatly to

the variety of its work. Meantime a large graduate school and a summer school of more than a thousand students have grown up. The course required for graduating has been extended in the Law School and the Dental School to three years and in the Medical School to four years of nine months each. The requirements for admission to the professional schools have been materially raised. Excellent hospitals for the use of the medical schools have been constructed and upon the highly advantageous plan of being entirely under the direction of the Medical Faculties. This allows students access to the patients with a freedom quite impossible in hospitals otherwise conducted. The idea of establishing hospitals on this basis originated here, and is now being adopted wherever practicable by medical schools.

It is not intended to give here a history of the University. But a few statistics may properly be given. There were three Departments in 1871; there are now seven. The members of the Faculties then numbered 35; now they are about 400. The students then numbered 1110; the last Calendar (1910–11) registered 5383. The libraries then contained 25,000 volumes; now they have 260,000. The income was then $104,000; now it is $1,170,000. The number of graduates from 1871 to 1909 is about 20,000, and the number of non-graduates approximately 17,000. They are found in every state and territory of the Union and on every continent of the globe.

My wife and I have received great pleasure in our home from the visits of distinguished men and women who have come to address the University. It seems proper to give reminiscences of some of these visits.

Matthew Arnold, in his last visit to America, accompanied by his wife and daughter, was our guest. It may be remembered that, when lecturing in the Eastern cities, he was criticized and even ridiculed for his manner of delivery. Being near-sighted, he had a reading-stand as tall as he was, and to his annoyance his manner in darting his head close to it at each sentence was compared to a bird pecking at his food. This fact led him, it was said, to take some lessons in elocution from a competent teacher. His appearance on our stage was one of the first after this instruction. He was received by our audience with great favour, and his success was so marked that he spoke to me with much satisfaction of his reception.

[249]

A business manager accompanied him on this Western tour. It was the custom of the railways in those days to give special rates to theatrical companies. Mr. Arnold told me with great glee that when the conductor of the train took the tickets from the manager, he exclaimed, "Oh! this is the Arnold troupe, is it?" He continued during his visit to address his wife and daughter as the Arnold troupe.

Having passed by Seneca Lake on his journey, he was apparently much interested in the fact that the lake bore the name of the great Roman philosopher. He was rather disappointed when I informed him that the lake took its name from the Seneca tribe of Indians and that the word Seneca is in that case of Indian origin.

Miss Edith Arnold, Mr. Arnold's niece, was my guest when she came to deliver a lecture on the Religious Novel. It was an address of high literary merit. She told me that a short time before his death Mr. Gladstone had a prolonged interview with her sister, Mrs. Humphrey Ward, in which he discussed at length with the author the religious doctrines set forth in the novel "Robert Elsmere." As Miss Arnold is a pronounced advocate of woman suffrage and Mrs. Ward is a leader on the other side, I asked her how they got on together in their consideration of that subject. "Oh," she said, "our difference does not in the least disturb our relations. For of course my sister does not understand the subject at all."

Dr. J. M. L. Curry, who was prominent on the Southern side in our Civil War and subsequently our Minister to Spain and Agent of the Peabody Education Fund for the aid of schools in the South, gave a very valuable Commencement Address for us. He and I sat up till midnight conversing on the race problems in the South. He manifested the most generous spirit towards the blacks. At last, after pacing the floor, he exclaimed with great fervour, striking the table with his hand, "We cannot see the whole of the future. But one thing we can know. It must be eternally right to educate the negro and to Christianize the negro." It is fortunate that so many Southerners have come to agree with him.

Among the many interesting stories he told of his experiences in travelling through the South, especially among the "poor whites," as they are called, of the mountain region between Virginia and Kentucky,

I venture to repeat this. In a very humble dwelling he noticed that the mother called her daughter who was waiting on the table "Ralgy." The name was so new to him that before he left he asked the mother where she found that name. In reply the woman brought an empty bottle which had contained patent medicine. She pointed to the label which announced that the medicine would cure *neuralgia* and other ailments. She thought neuralgia was a new and striking word, and so she had named the child "neuralgia," which in familiar address they had shortened to "Ralgy."

Henry M. Stanley, the African traveller, and his wife were most entertaining guests on the occasion of his visit here to lecture.

Our Law students have for many years celebrated Washington's birthday by securing an address from some eminent man. The February before Mr. Cleveland's second election to the Presidency, he was the orator of the day. I invited a number of the prominent citizens of both political parties to meet him at my house at luncheon. An immense throng from various parts of the State came to hear his address, which was very felicitous. In the evening a public reception was held by him in the city, and on the next evening another was held in Detroit. The result was that the Democratic party in Michigan raised with much spirit the cry for his nomination to the Presidency. And they have always boasted that the impulse thus given led to his nomination and election.

However that may be, his visit to Ann Arbor certainly had one result of some consequence. Years after I asked him how it happened that he chose for his permanent residence Princeton rather than New York. He replied, "When I visited Ann Arbor, you remember that you drove with me through several of the streets of your city. And when I saw so many modest and pleasant homes, I said to myself it is in a college town with its simple life that I will try to find a home when I am through with public life. I never lost sight of that thought. Hence my decision to live in Princeton rather than in New York."

One of my more recent visitors was the British Ambassador James Bryce, whose versatility was admirably displayed. In the evening he gave a most scholarly address to the Phi Beta Kappa Society on Culture. The next noon he addressed the Detroit Chamber of Commerce on Municipal Government, in which his great familiarity with municipal experiments and discussions, both European and American, appeared; in the evening he addressed the University Club in Detroit on the changes in American college and university life since his first visit to our country. In this address he showed a knowledge of our academic life that could not be surpassed by any of our college presidents. All these addresses were given without a scrap of paper before him. One was reminded of the offer ascribed to Mr. Carnegie to bet a million dollars that Mr. Bryce knows more than any other man in the world.

Many other eminent visitors might be named, among them Chinese and Japanese ambassadors, foreign missionaries, University Presidents, Mr. Justice Miller and Mr. Justice Harlan of the United States Supreme Court, Secretary Bayard, Mr. Roosevelt, when Governor of New York, Sir Frederick Pollock, and Charles A. Dana, editor of the New York *Sun*. These names may suffice to illustrate how stimulating the life of a University and especially the life in the President's home are made by the guests who come to lend inspiration to the Institution.

[254]

In considering the relation of the University to the State, I have always had two great ends in view.

First: I have endeavoured to induce every citizen to regard himself as a stockholder in the Institution, who had a real interest in helping make it of the greatest service to his children and those of his neighbours.

Secondly: I have sought to make all the schools and teachers in the State understand that they and the University are parts of one united system and that therefore the young pupil in the most secluded school house in the State should be encouraged to see that the path was open from his home up to and through the University.

The prosperity and usefulness of the University are due to the fact that these objects have been in a fair degree accomplished.

Although some State Universities were founded before ours, owing to the fact that the University of Michigan at an earlier date than any of the others secured a very large attendance in all three of its departments, its influence in the development of all the rest has been very great. No small portion of my correspondence has been devoted to explaining to other universities our methods and the reasons of our comparative success. I have been called to expound the principles on which Michigan has proceeded in building up its University to most of the States which have established their Universities.

Far be it from me to claim undue credit for the success of the Institution. Rather do I desire to speak of it with gratitude that I have been permitted to be so long associated with it in its days of prosperity. It has been a singular good fortune to be allowed to work with so many excellent men in the Board of Regents and in the Faculties and to come in touch with so many students who have gone forth to careers of usefulness in all parts of the world.

The life of the President of a college or university is often spoken of as a hard and trying life. A laborious life with its anxieties it is. But I have found it a happy life. The satisfactions it has brought to me are quite beyond my deserts. The recognition of the value of my services which has come to me in these recent days from regents, colleagues, graduates, and undergraduates humbles me while it gratifies me.

And one acknowledgment I desire above

all to make. If I have had any success in my career, especially in the administration of the two universities, it has been largely due to the social tact and wise and untiring co-operation of my dear wife.

In January, 1905, though not conscious that I had lost my physical or mental ability to discharge satisfactorily the duties of my office I tendered to the Regents my resignation, because I had observed that some men on reaching my age were not aware of infirmities which in the opinion of others disqualified them for continuing to hold responsible positions. The Board in very courteous terms declined to accept it.

But in February, 1909, having reached the age of fourscore, I renewed my request to be released under the conviction that notwithstanding the good health which had been granted to me, it was better for the University to call some younger man to my place. They kindly acceded to my request, asking me to accept the title of President Emeritus, to receive a generous salary, and to retain my residence in the President's house. I cannot be too grateful for what they have done to cheer my pathway through the remaining years of my life. I can thus hope to spend the days allotted

[257]

to me near to them, to my beloved colleagues in the Faculties, and to the great
company of students whose presence has
long been, and still is, one of my great
delights.

THE END